D1610029

DAVITT

1. *Michael Davitt in 1904, two years before his death.*

DAVITT

Bernard O'Hara

Mayo County Council

Published by: Mayo County Council,
                       Áras an Chontae,
                       Castlebar,
                       County Mayo,
                       Ireland.

In association with: The Michael Davitt Memorial Association,
                       Straide,
                       County Mayo,
                       Ireland.

AJF   941.5081092 | 20004003267446

Leabharlanna Chonndae Phortláirge

ISBN   0 9519624 77

British Library Cataloguing in Publication Data

A CIP catalogue record for this book can be obtained from the British Library.

Printed by: Berry Print Group,
                       Westport,
                       County Mayo.

For my wife, Mary, and our family.

CONTENTS

ILLUSTRATIONS

PREFACE

Since earliest childhood, Michael Davitt was the historical giant at my shoulder. Growing up in County Mayo, 'The Father of the Land League' was revered there. Widely acknowledged as a hero of the Irish race long before his death, Michael Davitt has a secure place in the history of his country and is rightly seen as one of its greatest patriots. This book is intended as a concise illustrated biography of Michael Davitt for the general reader, written in the context of the main developments of his floruit.

It was written chiefly from secondary sources, especially three of his biographers: Dr T. W. Moody, Carla King and Francis Sheehy-Skeffington. The chief source was Dr T. W. Moody's *Davitt and Irish Revolution 1846-82*, an excellent contextual study of the first thirty-six years of Michael Davitt's life, with a summary of the last twenty-four included in the final chapter. Where there were differences in facts and dates with other sources, the versions in Dr Moody's work were followed. He also published a number of interesting articles on various aspects of Michael Davitt's life and some complement the material covered in the last chapter of his book.

Dr Carla King, the most recent Davitt scholar, published a short biography, *Michael Davitt*, in 1999, which is well researched and written. She also edited and published some of the material written by Michael Davitt in Portland Prison in *Jottings in Solitary* (2003), as well as his books and some of his other writing in *Michael Davitt: Collected Writings 1868-1906* (2001). She is working on the Davitt papers in Trinity College, Dublin, and writing a biography on the later life of Michael Davitt, which is expected to complement the excellent work done by T. W. Moody. Even then, many of Davitt's activities provide fertile ground for more scholarship.

Michael Davitt: Revolutionary, Agitator and Labour Leader by Francis Sheehy-Skeffington, published in 1908, contains much interesting material on Davitt's life but it is strongly influenced by his own socialist, nationalistic and anti-clerical views.

Michael Davitt's own books provided many sources especially *Leaves from a Prison Diary*, *Defence of his Land League* and *The Fall of Feudalism in Ireland*. F. S. L. Lyons's *Ireland Since the Famine* and Joseph J. Lee's *The Modernisation of Irish Society, 1848-1918*, were indispensable texts for the general period, while *Land and Popular Politics in Ireland: County Mayo from the Plantation to the Land War* by Donald E. Jordan Jr. provided a interesting analysis of County Mayo from before the Great Famine up to and including the end of the land war in 1882.

I would like to record my gratitude to the late Cahir and Dr. Robert Davitt, sons of Michael, for their letters on a number of issues and the help provided by Grainne Davitt, a granddaughter and Fr Thomas Davitt, CM, a grandson. Their replies to various queries were much appreciated.

A sincere thanks is due to Nancy Smyth, chairperson of the Michael Davitt Memorial Association, for all her interest and help. She wrote 'An Outline History of the Michael Davitt Memorial Association' which is published in appendix 1. My sincere thanks to all the people who supplied photographs for publication, especially the Michael Davitt Memorial Museum, Straide, most of which came from members of the Davitt family, as well as from Nancy Smyth, John Garavan, Dr Mark Garavan and Fintan Coogan. My thanks are due to the staff of the Michael Davitt Memorial Museum especially, Mary Lawless, Peggy Boyle, John Geraghty and Joseph Yeomans.

I am deeply indebted to Peadar O'Dowd and Dr. John Hynes, Galway-Mayo Institute of Technology (GMIT), and Dr Nollaig Ó Muraíle, National University of Ireland, Galway, for reading the first draft of this book and giving me their critical comments that enhanced the final outcome. I alone am responsible for any errors that remain. My sincere thanks are due to Mary Kennedy, Galway-Mayo Institute of Technology, and Eileen O'Hara, Killasser, County Mayo, for their help. Thanks are also due to the staff of the library in GMIT especially Margaret Waldron, Bernie Lally, Marie Barrett and Antionette O'Malley, to Cian Marnell and James O'Connor, GMIT, to Thomas Hennigan and Mícheál Murphy, Killasser, to Matt Moran, a former chairperson of the Michael Davitt Memorial Association, as well as to Donal and Teresa Downes, Galway.

I am deeply grateful to Mayo County Council for publishing this book, to its Cathaoirleach, Henry Kenny, for writing the Introduction, to the County Manager, Des Mahon, for his support, to Austin Vaughan, County Librarian, as well as Ivor Hamrock and Maureen Costello for all their help. Sincere thanks are also due to the staff of Berry Print Group, Westport, especially Maria Moran, Michael McLoughlin and Seán McCormack. Finally, I would like to thank my wife, Mary, for all her understanding, help and support while this book was being written.

Bernard O'Hara
30 May 2006

INTRODUCTION

Is mór an onóir dom, mar Chathaoirleach Chomhairle Contae Mhaigh Eo, an réamhrá a scríobh le haghaidh an leabhair seo faoi Mhícheál Mac Dáibhéid. Tá Comhairle Contae Mhaigh Eo an-sásta an leabhar seo a fhoilsiú i gcuimhne ar Éireannach mór le rá a bhfuil comóradh céad bliain a bháis ann i mbliana. Táim fíorbhuíoch de Bhearnard Ó hEaghra as an leabhar breá seo a scríobh agus as comhoibriú leis an gComhairle Contae maidir lena fhoilsiú.

Michael Davitt is one of the giants in Irish history and it is most appropriate that his native county remembers him this year on the centenary of his death. His love for his native place could not be expressed more eloquently then by his wish to be buried in Straide. The publication of this book is one of a number of activities being organised in his honour by Mayo County Council in this centenary year. Michael Davitt was the founder, organiser, and inspiring leader of the Land League, which fundamentally changed the social structure of rural Ireland within a generation, with the conversion of tenant farmers into occupying-owners and the replacement of the landlord class. It became the greatest social revolution ever witnessed in Ireland and led to independence as well as the foundation of a modern democracy. While the land agitation was started in County Mayo by James Daly and others, Michael Davitt became its architect-in-chief, developing a local protest into a national movement, linked to the Irish Parliamentary Party in the House of Commons. After serving over seven years' penal servitude for his Fenian activities, Michael Davitt emerged without rancour or vindictiveness towards any person, but with a burning desire to see the landlord system replaced.

While his name will always be synonymous with the Land League, he was involved in an astonishing variety of other activities, journalist, author, patron of the GAA, nationalist leader, pioneer of the Labour movement, and Home Rule MP. All these aspects of his life and more are covered in this illustrated, well-researched, and well-written book. Starting with the origin of the Irish land question, the book traces Michael Davitt's life from his birth in Straide, to his eviction, emigration and youth in an English industrial town. This is followed by his Fenian activities, his arrest, trial and imprisonment. Michael Davitt's role in bringing about a 'new departure' in Fenian policy is explained, as well as the origin, development and end of the Land League. The slow process which led to the tenant-farmers becoming owners of the land, and the final settlement of the land annuities dispute with Britain in 1938, are then described. The book covers Davitt's support for land nationalisation and Home Rule, his estrangement from Parnell, as well as his political activities and pioneering role in the labour movement. His death, will, and funeral to Straide are all described. The final chapter contains a review of the Land League, and Davitt's role in it, as well as his personal qualities and place in history. He is one of the most loved figures in Irish history and his qualities of selflessness and integrity serve as a wonderful role model for the Irish of today. County Mayo is proud of Michael Davitt's enormous achievements for his native country and indeed for the many causes he championed around the world. By the end of his life he was a well-known and respected international figure.

On behalf of Mayo County Council, I would like to sincerely thank Bernard O'Hara for writing this very impressive book. He has already written extensively about various aspects of the history and heritage of County Mayo and I am deeply grateful to him for undertaking this project. I would also like to record my appreciation to the staff of the Mayo County Library for co-operating with Bernard in the publication of the book.

Finally, I wish to record my gratitude to all the present and former members of the Michael Davitt Memorial Association for their ongoing work in ensuring Davitt's memory is preserved and especially to Nancy Smyth, the current chairperson.

Is beathaisnéis é seo atá dea-scríofa agus a bhfuil léaráidí breátha ann. Fáiltím roimh an leabhar agus mholfainn do dhuine ar bith a bhfuil suim aige nó aici i stair ár dtíre é a léamh.

Henry Kenny,
Cathaoirleach Chomhairle Contae Mhaigh Eo.

1

Introduction: The Irish Land Question

Michael Davitt (1846-1906), 'The Father of the Land League', social reformer, Member of Parliament, author, Gaelic Athletic Association patron, pioneer of the Labour movement and international humanitarian, was County Mayo's most famous son and one of Ireland's greatest patriots. He was the founder and master organiser of the Land League, one of the most successful movements in Irish history, which transformed tenant farmers into owner-occupiers within a generation by constitutional means, and in the process brought about one of the greatest social changes ever witnessed in Ireland. His sympathy and concern ranged from Irish tenant farmers to agricultural labourers, the plight of the British working-class, prison reform, social reform, the Boers in South Africa, and the Jews in Russia. A champion of the oppressed and exploited, Michael Davitt also worked for an independent, democratic, Irish State. T. W. Moody, professor of history in the University of Dublin from 1939 to 1977 and author of the seminal work, *Davitt and Irish Revolution 1846–1882*,[1] wrote of Michael Davitt:

> He served his fellow men under the impulsion not of any dogma but of a generous
> and compassionate spirit that surmounted all distinctions of class and circumstances
> no less than of religion and national origin.[2]

To understand the transformation brought about in land ownership, it is necessary to consider the origin of the Irish Land question, which with Home Rule became the big political issues in nineteenth century Ireland.

Conquest

There was a widespread decentralised clan structure in ancient Ireland, operating under a legal code known as the Brehon Laws. Land belonged to the clan and there was little private property in the modern sense. This system came under growing pressure in the aftermath of the Norman invasion in the twelfth century.

After the defeat of the armies of Gaelic Ulster and their Spanish allies at the Battle of Kinsale in 1601 and the Flight of the Earls in 1607, the old Gaelic civilisation went into rapid decline. Rebellions, land confiscations, and plantations of the sixteenth and the seventeenth centuries changed land ownership in large parts of Ireland. The amount of land owned by Catholics (both Gaelic and 'old English' origin) declined from over sixty per cent in 1641 to under twenty per cent at the end of the century and that figure was reduced still further in the course of the eighteenth century. Arising from the confiscations and plantations, the land came into the ownership of landlords, who let it to a large number of tenant farmers on leases and tenancies. While land-ownership changed, occupancy, in most cases, remained the same.

By the start of the nineteenth century, two distinct social groups had emerged in Ireland: English–speaking Protestant landlords (some of them Catholics who changed religion to keep their property during the penal laws) with large estates, and mainly Catholic, many of them Gaelic-speaking, tenant farmers, together with landless cottiers and agricultural labourers. The landlords were seen as the successors of those who received confiscated land and the tenant farmers as the descendants of those who were defeated and lost their lands. As a consequence, tenant farmers and their families resented the landlord class, but it was not a major issue while they and other social groups dependent on them were able to make a reasonable living. The landlords fixed rents arbitrarily, with no relation to price changes or economic conditions. Secret societies of tenants and their supporters, which were established in various areas during the late eighteenth century and the early decades of the following one, became involved in agrarian agitation, often resulting in violence and intimidation, especially at eviction scenes or at any perceived exploitation of tenant farmers.

Landlord Class

Many landlords, resident and absentees, were progressive and energetic in the development of their estates and surrounding districts, and some of them built well-planned towns and villages to serve as commercial centres. Some landlords were to earn reputations as unproductive, uncaring and exploitative. The landlords were the

2. *Eviction scene 1767.*

2. *Eviction scene 1777*

backbone of the ascendancy class in Ireland and different from most of their Irish tenants in many ways: religion, politics, education, traditions, culture and often in language. They held exclusive rights as legislators and as administrators, with Irish Members of Parliament coming from the landlord class and at county level controlling the grand juries, bodies that provided a local government service and ruled on the validity of indictments at local assizes. Members of grand juries were selected by the High Sheriff from the leading landlords in each county, with the class who made the laws also providing the magistrates to enforce them. Some inroads were made on this privileged class by the growth of democracy and reform measures in the early nineteenth century, as well as losing some power when Daniel O'Connell (1775–1847) won Catholic Emancipation in 1829, enabling Catholics to enter parliament as well as holding civil and military offices. Greater erosion of landlord power took place with the growth of central State administration than by any advance in the position of Irish tenant farmers. However, the steps towards democracy were slow.

Tenant Farmers

Tenant farmers and dependent classes were not a homogeneous group. There were some on long-term leases, middlemen, farmers with short-term tenancies of usually a year or 'at-will', as well as cottiers and agricultural labourers. Some tenants held long-term leases but, because of the penal laws, these were mainly Protestants. There were middlemen operating on various estates who acted as agents for landlords and sub-let land, usually on short-term leases or tenancies. Some tenant farmers had big holdings, but the vast majority occupied small farms on short-term tenancies and could be evicted after receiving six months' notice to quit.

Cottiers generally worked for tenant farmers and, as payment, received cabins and small plots on which they grew potatoes for their families and had some grazing rights for a cow and other stock. In addition, they sometimes had the use of commonage for grazing livestock and the right to cut turf on a bog, with some of them able to earn supplementary money from their employers or as migrant labourers. Cottiers were numerous in the early decades of the nineteenth century and provided cheap labour for the labour-intensive farming of that period. Agricultural labourers, who worked for the landlords and the bigger tenant farmers, were also numerous. Some had full-time work, but the vast majority were hired for seasonal or daily employment, receiving a potato plot and a cabin in return for specific work. Many also took some conacre: land rented from landlords or tenant farmers for eleven months each season.

The living conditions of agricultural labourers, cottiers, and numerous farmers with smallholdings were dreadful during the early years of the nineteenth century.[3] In 1841, about thirty-seven per cent of all Irish houses were classified as fourth class, mud cabins with one room, and forty per cent as third class, mud cabins with two to four rooms and windows. Conditions deteriorated with a big growth in population, bad harvests and fluctuating incomes, with sub-division of land to eligible children leading to progressive impoverishment. There was a big deterioration in landlord/tenant relations and increased friction between tenant farmers, cottiers and agricultural labourers. Most farmers were forced by their precarious financial situations to become tenants-at-will with no security of tenure for any period, which exacerbated their circumstances. For over half the population of Ireland the land question was a matter of survival, especially in Connacht.

The Great Famine

Early in the nineteenth century, there were a number of regional famines in Ireland, culminating in the Great Famine of 1845–1849, when an estimated million people died and a further million went into exile. The population increased from about four and a half million in 1800 to over eight million by 1841. The pressure of this vast increase exacerbated the fragile subsistence economy of the period, as land became subdivided into smaller and smaller plots. In 1841, forty-five per cent of all farms were less than five acres and in Connacht the figure was sixty-four per cent.[4] Destitution was already a fact of life for many and evictions became regular occurrences in the Irish countryside. Emigration on a large scale took place before the Great Famine, while seasonal migration helped numerous families to survive. Most of the impoverished population depended on the potato as their staple food product because of its nutritional value and high productivity (a small plot could produce enough potatoes to feed a large family for a year).

Disaster struck in August 1845, when a killer fungus, later identified as *phytophthora infestans,* started to destroy the potato crop. The green stalks of potato ridges became blighted and within a short time were producing a terrible stench. About a third of the national potato crop was destroyed that year, and an almost complete failure the following year led to a catastrophe for the remainder of the decade. By 'black forty-seven', people were dying in their thousands from starvation-related diseases. The workhouses, built in the early 1840s to relieve appalling poverty, were unable to cope with the numbers seeking admission and various parsimonious relief measures were inadequate to deal with the scale of the crisis.

The number of evictions increased, with this process of 'clearance' (as it was called) aided by the 'quarter-acre clause' (the infamous 'Gregory clause', called after its proposer, Sir William Gregory, MP, of Coole Park, Co. Galway) in the Poor Law Extension Act 1847, which excluded from relief anyone who had more than a quarter acre of land. Any unfortunate person who was starving had to abandon his holding and go to the workhouse if he and his family wanted a chance to survive. Conditions became worse in 1848 and 1849, with contemporary reports recording dead bodies everywhere.[5]

The catastrophe was particularly bad in County Mayo, where nearly ninety per cent of the population were dependent on the potato. By 1848, Mayo was a county of total misery and despair, with any attempts at alleviating measures in complete disarray, and people were dying and emigrating in their thousands. We will never know how many died in the county during those terrible years: statistics show that the population dropped from 388,887 in 1841 to 274,499 in 1851.[6]

'The Great Clearances'

The cottier and agricultural labouring classes were decimated, with thousands dying and emigrating: numbers fell from over one million in 1845 to approximately 700,000 by 1851 and continued to decline for many decades. Small-farmers also suffered considerably. Table 1 shows the impact of the Great Famine on various social strata with land holdings between 1841 and 1851.[7] There was a huge reduction in the number of holdings under five acres (2.2 hectares), falling from about forty-five per cent of the total in 1841 to just over fifteen per cent in 1851, because they could not support a family. Holdings over fifteen acres (six hectares) increased, creating more economic units. During that period, the number of farms over thirty acres (12.14 hectares) increased from seven per cent of the total to twenty-six per cent. The total number of holdings in Ireland fell from 691,202 in 1841 to 570,338 in 1851, a decline of 120,864 or 17.48 per cent. The practice of land sub-division came to an end, and thereafter one son generally inherited the full holding, but he had often to wait for years before parents transferred their rights.

Table 1: Land Holdings in Ireland 1841-1851				
Holdings	**1841**	**Per Cent**	**1851**	**Per Cent**
1 - 5 acres	310,436	44.9	88,083	15.5
5 - 15 acres	252,799	36.6	191,854	33.6
15 - 30 acres	79,342	11.5	141,311	24.8
Above 30 acres	48,625	7.0	149,090	26.1

Source: Ó Tuathaigh, Gearóid, *Ireland Before the Famine*, page 206.

The landlord class was not immune from loss. With the increasing burden of the poor rates to help the destitute and numerous tenants unable to pay their rents, the incomes of many landlords declined rapidly: some became insolvent. The Encumbered Estates Court was established in 1849 to facilitate the sale of insolvent estates, with about one-seventh of the land of Ireland sold in the decade after the Great Famine.

Numerous tenant farmers had big rent arrears, and this resulted in mass evictions during what were called 'the great clearances' from 1849 to 1853, when almost 47,000 families and 239,413 people were evicted,[8] a huge number of dispossessed people. Some of these evictions were carried out by the new owners of estates who had purchased them through the Encumbered Estates Court. The landlords carried out the evictions to recover some of their land from small farmers who were unable to pay the rents and arrears as well as from cottiers who were destitute. The changes brought about in land holdings during the Great Famine and 'the great clearances' were cataclysmic, but they created better conditions for those who remained. The harrowing experience of the Great Famine period left bitter memories with those who survived and the psychological impact lasted for life. As Ireland was then part of the British Empire, memories of the Great Famine created anti-British feeling in the country and among Irish emigrants, as well as considerable resentment against the landlord system.

Among the casualties of 'the great clearances' was the family of a child from Straide, County Mayo; Michael Davitt was never to forget that trauma: hence his burning ambition to change the landlord system.

1

References and Notes

1. *Davitt and Irish Revolution 1846–82*, Oxford University Press, 1981, is the authoritative work on the first thirty-six years of Michael Davitt's life. It is the main source used for this publication. T. W. Moody was given Michael Davitt's private and unpublished material by his daughter, Eileen. They are now in the Davitt papers in Trinity College, Dublin. The collection also contains over 500 photographs. A full description of the Davitt papers can be obtained in the *List of Davitt Papers*, 26 July 1999, in the TCD Manuscripts Library.
    (T. W. Moody died in Dublin on 11 February 1984, aged 76.)
2. 'Michael Davitt', in Boyle, J. W., (ed.), *Leaders and Workers*, p. 55.
3. Swords, Liam, *A Dominant Church*, chapter 4.
4. Green, E.R.R., 'The Great Famine', in Moody, T. W. and Martin, F. X., *The Course of Irish History*, p. 267.
5. *Ibid.*
6. Census of Population.
7. Ó Tuathaigh, Gearóid, *Ireland Before the Famine*, p. 206.
    Note: To convert acres to hectares, multiply by 0.4047.
8. Moody, T.W., *Davitt and Irish Revolution 1849-82*, appendix D, p. 562.

2

Background and Fenian Involvement

Straide (alias Strade on ordnance survey maps) is one of twenty-seven townlands in the parish of Templemore, now generally known as Straide, in County Mayo. The population of the parish fell from 4,251 in 1841 to 2,387 in 1851, a reduction of 43.8 per cent, while the townland of Straide declined from 321 to 236, or 26.47 per cent, and the number of houses from 60 to 45.[1] Like the rest of the county, Straide was a place of poverty, death, emigration and misery during the Great Famine.

Straide is a historic parish. Straide friary was founded under the patronage of Jordan de Exeter around 1240 for the Franciscans, but at the insistence of his daughter-in-law, Basilia Bermingham, it was transferred to the Dominicans in 1252.[2] The surviving structure has a thirteenth-century chancel with six small lancet windows, but the rest of the building dates from a fifteenth-century restoration. Its two treasures date from the restoration: a high altar with elegant decorations including a Pieta flanked by donors, and the delightfully sculptured founder's tomb with flamboyant tracery.[3] The ruin of the thirteenth-century Jordan de Exeter's castle at Ballylahan can be seen about two kilometres to the north-west on the right of the road to Foxford near the river Moy. Ashbrook House is another local historic building, the ancestral home of the Moore family of Moore Hall. George Moore, who was born in Ashbrook, went to Spain and became a wealthy merchant in the wine trade in Alicante before returning in 1792 to build Moore Hall near the shore of Lough Carra in 1796. His son, John, was appointed

3. *The surviving structure of Straide Friary.*

President of the 'Republic of Connacht' on 31 August 1798 after General Humbert and the French/Irish forces captured Castlebar following the landing of the French in Killala Bay. Regardless of its other connections, Straide is chiefly known today in Irish history as the birthplace of Michael Davitt.

Family and Eviction

Michael Davitt was born at the height of the Great Famine, on 25 March 1846, near the friary in Straide, County Mayo, the second child of Martin Davitt and his wife, Catherine.[4] Martin, who was born in or around 1814 probably in the townland of Straide, became a yearly tenant farmer on the estate of John Knox.[5] As a young person, Martin was involved in a local agrarian secret society during the 1830s and, arising from these activities, he went to England for a period before returning to Straide to farm a small holding of land.[6] Martin, who probably attended a local hedge-school in his youth, was literate, bi-lingual, and a good reader, with a big interest in Irish and American history. He had a reputation as a good *seanchaí*, or storyteller, and in later years Michael remembered his narratives of the French landing in Killala Bay on 22 August 1798 to support a rebellion in Ireland, accounts of the Great Famine, and other events in Irish history. These stories were to nurture strong patriotic feelings in Michael as well as a dislike of the landlord system.[7] The exact date of Martin's marriage to Catherine is not known, but it was probably in or around 1840.

Catherine Davitt, *née* Kielty, was born around 1820 beside the round tower in the townland of Turlough in a parish of the same name in County Mayo. She could neither read nor write, which was very common at that time, but was the dominant partner in the marriage.[8] A fluent Irish speaker, she had a great pride in the language as almost all families in County Mayo were then Irish speaking. As a lover of the Irish language, she regularly closed discussions with an apt Gaelic proverb like: *Is fearr clú ná conách* (character is better than wealth).[9] Catherine, passionate, proud, and possessed of a great natural intelligence, was a good Christian, with a rich imagination, strong nationalistic views and a good memory, especially of the suffering and poverty she and her family endured. Her stories of these times were very influential on Michael.

Four children were born to Martin and Catherine Davitt in Straide: Mary (1841), Michael (1846), Anne (1848) and Sabina (1850).[10] (A fifth child was later born in England but did not

4. *Catherine Davitt,* née *Kielty, Michael Davitt's mother.*

survive.) They were christened in the nearby seventeenth-century church in Straide (which was refurbished and opened in 2000 to house the Michael Davitt museum). The late 1840s was a difficult period in which to rear a young family. With the frugal subsistence of most families deteriorating each year, it was a major struggle to survive. Despite securing work on a local relief scheme and going to England as a seasonal migratory labourer for the summer of 1849, Martin Davitt was unable to pay off the arrears of rent which had accumulated during the Great Famine. After being served with an ejectment notice in 1849, the Davitt family were evicted, probably in October 1850, as part of the 'great clearances.' This involved the landlord's agents forcing in the door of their home with a battering ram, putting the family out on the road, and knocking the house, an unforgettable experience for any family. Michael Davitt described the scene many years later:

> I was then but four and a half years old, yet I have a distinct remembrance (doubtless strengthened by the frequent narration of the event by my parents in after years) of that morning's scene: the remnant of our household furniture flung about the road; the roof of the house falling in and the thatch taking fire; my mother and father looking on with four young children, the youngest only two months old, adding their cries to the other pangs which must have agitated their souls at the sight of their burning homestead.[11]

The family went to the workhouse in Swinford, but when Catherine Davitt was told that male children over three years of age had to be separated from their mothers, she promptly took her family away after one hour.[12] The Davitt family, like others during that period, felt that entering the workhouse was the nadir of degradation. Michael later recalled in his writings that he never once heard his father refer to the incident but that his mother, who had great respect for the truth, often did.

5. *The only surviving section of Swinford workhouse.*

Emigration

Sharing the fate of many thousands of Irish dispossessed by the famine, the Davitt family emigrated to Haslingden, a small textile town in Lancashire, about twenty-seven kilometres north of Manchester. They were transported to Dublin by another family from the vicinity of Straide who were going by horse and cart in return for the promise of a future payment. They then crossed to Liverpool and stayed with some friends for a few days before making the twenty-seven kilometre journey to Haslingden by foot. After securing temporary accommodation with an acquaintance, the Davitt family were asked to leave after two nights when it was learned that Michael had measles. They stayed in a makeshift tent until another family gave them accommodation. Later they stayed with friends, the family of Owen Eagan, in Wilkinson Street until they were able to rent a house of their own nearby at Rock Hall on a slope of Cribden Hill at the north-east of the town.[13] (The terrace of small houses where Michael Davitt lived was demolished years ago.) It was in Rock Hall that their fifth child and Michael's only brother, James, was born in June 1853 (he died two years later).[14] Martin's first job was selling fruit from door to door, and he later became a labourer. It was here Michael spent his youth in difficult circumstances, but as a member of a loving family in a Gaelic colony of an English industrial town.

Rock Hall had a small, closely-knit, Irish community, with regular entertainment in music, *céilithe*, and story-telling, especially about social conditions in Ireland and the injustice of the landlord system. Martin and Catherine Davitt played big roles in the story telling. Michael Davitt, many years later, told *The Times*-Parnell Commission (1889) that he recalled many a time in their English home listening to his mother's stories of the famine years. One story made a very big impression on his young mind. He told the Commission that he remembered hearing from his mother a graphic account of how three hundred poor people who had died of starvation round where he was born, between Straide and Swinford, had been thrown into one pit in the corner of the workhouse yard in Swinford:

> without coffin, without sermon, without anything which denotes respect for the dead. So great an impression did this make upon me in my youthful days in Lancashire that when I visited Swinford twenty-five years afterwards, I went to the very spot where these bodies had been buried without asking anyone to direct me to the place.[15]

6. *The entrance to the mass famine grave in Swinford.*

Arm Amputated

Martin Davitt, who had a reputation of being a scholar, helped some local children to read and write, as there was no compulsory schooling at that time. Michael attended an infants' school, which opened in Wilkinson Street in 1854, for one year until 1855. By his own wish at the age of nine, Michael decided to become a wage-earner so as to help the finances of his family, and commenced employment in a local cotton mill at Ewood Bridge owned by John Parkinson, where he worked sixty hours a week for 2s 6d a week.[16] After a month, he resigned and spent a short period with another employer, Lawrence Whittaker, before taking a job in Stellfoxe's Victoria Mill, at Baxenden outside Haslingden. There, on 8 May 1857, his right arm was badly injured by a machine, due to the negligence of the employer and supervisor.[17] After being taken home on a cart, leaving a trail of blood along the road, Michael had to be chloroformed by force for the amputation of his right arm just below the shoulder.[18] This was a major tragedy for an eleven year old. At that time, work in the Lancashire cotton mills was a hazardous and cruel experience for children, with dangerous equipment like exposed shafts and cogwheels often left unguarded, and it was not unusual to see supervisors bully children around the mills. Deaths and maiming at work were common occurrences and compensation did not exist. The accident ended Michael's employment for four years and left him with a deep life-long understanding of and sympathy for industrial workers.

When he had recovered from the operation, his parents, with help from a local cotton-manufacturer and benefactor, John Dean, were able to send him back to school for four years.[19] He went to the local Wesleyan school in Chapel Street, which was connected to

7. *Stellfoxe's Victoria Mill, Baxenden, near Haslingden, where Michael Davitt lost his right arm on 8 May 1857. The actual building was demolished in the nineteen-sixties.*

the Methodist Church and recommended by his parish priest, Rev. Thomas Martin, a liberal-minded man who believed strongly in inter-denominational harmony.[20] It was an ecumenical school, conducted by George Poskett, where Michael did not hear one word that hurt his feelings as a Catholic. He saw and accepted religious differences, and throughout his life never showed any trace of sectarian bigotry.

Michael took up employment in 1861 with Henry Cockcroft, who ran the post-office in Haslingden alongside a printing business. Michael was a very loyal, able and reliable worker in a variety of jobs, including messenger, printer's devil, typesetter and bookkeeper.[21] In 1858, Michael started attending evening classes in the local Mechanics' Institute, where he made regular use of the library and a newsroom that had the main newspapers and periodicals in Britain.[22] He was very impressed by the opportunities provided by the Institute for working people to improve their education by evening study. The Davitt family left Rock Hall in 1867 and returned to Wilkinson Street, which was their home until they emigrated to the United States. (There is a wall memorial in Wilkinson Street, which marks the site of the home of Michael Davitt.)

8. *The former post office building in Haslingden, where Michael Davitt worked from 1861 to 1868.*

Irish Republican Brotherhood

After the Act of Union came into effect on 1 January 1801, all of Ireland was part of the United Kingdom of Great Britain and Ireland until the establishment of the Irish Free State in 1922. From the middle of the nineteenth century, there was considerable animosity within Ireland to the union because of the Great Famine, and the belief that in an independent State more would have been done to ameliorate the situation. Two strong strands developed within Irish nationalism: constitutional methods to address grievances, inspired by Daniel O'Connell, and physical force. Both strands sought self-government for Ireland, but the constitutionalists would accept domestic rule within the union, while the other strand desired complete national independence. In Ulster, where nearly half the population were descendants of English and Scottish settlers, there was strong support for remaining in the union.

On St. Patrick's Day 1858, James Stephens (1824-1901) formally constituted in Dublin a movement that emerged as a secret conspiratorial oath-bound revolutionary society and became known as the Irish Republican Brotherhood (IRB), or the Fenians, named after the warriors of ancient Ireland. The name came from a parallel branch of the organisation that was started in America by John O'Mahony (1816-'77) and Michael Doheny (1805-'63). The objective of the organisation was to overthrow British rule in Ireland by force and establish a democratic Irish republic. It grew rapidly and recruited widely in Ireland, England and America. As a separatist revolutionary body, the leaders of the IRB despised those who favoured constitutional politics and feared that any co-operation with them would weaken orthodox Fenian policy. Members of the IRB swore 'allegiance to the Irish republic now virtually established.' The politics of the 1860s did not bring any improvements for tenant farmers, as it was a period of political opportunism, corruption and cynicism, with growing support for the Fenians. Nevertheless, an attempted rising in 1867 was a fiasco.

A Fenian

Michael Davitt joined the Irish Republican Brotherhood in Haslingden during 1865 with the full knowledge and support of his parents.[23] Given his background and the attitude of the Irish community in industrial Lancashire where he spent his formative years, it was easy for a patriotic and idealistic young Irishman like Michael Davitt to be influenced to join the Fenians.

After a short time, he was elected 'centre' of the Rossendale 'circle' of the IRB, effectively the leader of about fifty members. He combined his work in Cockcroft's with his Fenian activities for a period of two years, and took part in an abortive attempt to seize arms stored in Chester Castle on 11 February 1867, his only Fenian military operation.[24] He and his comrades withdrew after they heard that the authorities had become aware of the plan through an informer and were awaiting their arrival. In 1868, Michael helped defend St. Mary's Catholic Church on the Bury Road in Haslingden against an attack by some Protestant bigots. He and his three sisters had been confirmed at the first such ceremony in St. Mary's Church on 22 September 1861.[25]

In 1868, Michael Davitt became organising secretary and arms' agent for the IRB in England and Scotland, a position that involved regular contact between the Fenians in Britain and the supreme council of the IRB.[26] The following year, he resigned from his employment in Cockcroft's to work full-time on his Fenian activities and, as a cover for his operations, he assumed the role of a commercial traveller dealing in firearms.[27] He established a store in Leeds for his work under the name of Robert Jackson.[28] The position involved a lot of travel, and he became involved in arms traffic to Ireland.

9. *St. Mary's Catholic Church, Haslingden, where Michael Davitt was confirmed on 22 September 1861. (A tablet and organ in memory of him were erected in this church in February 1908).*

Family leave for America

Michael Davitt's eldest sister, Mary, married a Mayo-man from the Attymass/ Kilgarvan area, Neil Padden, on 16 May 1863 at St Mary's Catholic Church in Haslingden.[29] Shortly afterwards, Neil emigrated to the United States and ended up in Scranton, an industrial town in the north-east of Pennsylvania, and Mary joined him there in June 1865. Having regard to his Fenian activities, Michael persuaded his parents and other sisters, Anne and Sabina, to emigrate to Mary and Neil Padden in the United States.[30] It was their wish to return to Ireland if they could make a living there, but acceding to Michael's pressure they decided to emigrate to America. Preceded by Anne and Sabina, Martin and Catherine Davitt sailed from Liverpool and arrived in New York on 13 April 1870, from where they went to Scranton.[31] (They were never to see Ireland or England again, which was the experience of almost all emigrants at that time.)

10. *Michael Davitt as a young man.*

Trial for Treason-Felony

Police informers, who were liable to be killed if discovered, infiltrated the IRB. In December 1869, a Manchester Fenian, Arthur Forrester, told Michael Davitt that he suspected a Fenian named Burke to be a spy and wanted to take action against him. Davitt asked for some proof of the allegation, which Forrester was unable to provide. Later, Forrester informed Davitt that he had obtained proof and called for the informer to be killed. Davitt, in an effort to stop the proposed killing, wrote to Forrester as if he agreed with him but asked that no action be taken until he had obtained the authority of members of the supreme council of the IRB.[32] Unfortunately for Davitt, while this so-called 'pen' letter was intended to prevent murder, it appeared to support it.[33] After the police discovered the letter, it resulted in increased surveillance on his activities and its use in a later trial. After months of surveillance, Michael Davitt and a gunsmith with whom he was dealing, named John Wilson, were arrested separately at Paddington railway station in London on 14 May 1870 and charged with treason-felony.[34]

Their trial took place in the Old Bailey in London in July 1870 before Lord Chief Justice Sir Alexander Cockburn and a jury. Forrester's appearance as a witness for the defence regarding the famous letter did considerable harm; far more than the evidence of an informer, John Joseph Coryden, an ex-Fenian who had provided information on the Chester Castle plan, for the prosecution. Both defendants were found guilty of arms trafficking to Ireland for a Fenian insurrection. Wilson claimed that he did not know that the arms were going to Ireland or that he was doing anything wrong. Davitt made an impassioned appeal on behalf of Wilson, offering to take any punishment given to Wilson in addition to his own so that he did not suffer. While the Chief Justice was impressed by Davitt's plea, he could not accept that Wilson did not know the use to which the arms might be put and sentenced him to seven years. The plea had a mitigating influence for Wilson, but Michael Davitt was sentenced on 18 July 1870 to fifteen years' penal servitude.[35] While guilty of the offence, he was unlucky to have been convicted on the basis of the evidence presented at the trial.

Penal Servitude

At the age of twenty-four, Michael Davitt responded to the third great challenge of his life (after his eviction and the loss of his right arm) with characteristic fortitude. After his conviction, he was removed to Millbank Penitentiary in London, where he was put in solitary confinement and employed in oakum picking.[36] On 25 May 1871, he was transferred to Dartmoor prison in Devon, the toughest in Britain, where he remained until his release in 1877, except for a period of a month in 1872 that was spent in Portsmouth prison. His prison accommodation was a small corrugated-iron cell with inadequate light or ventilation, and he often had to kneel with his mouth to an opening at the bottom of his cell door to get some air. Work involved stone-breaking, being attached to a gang hauling a cart around the prison yard, pounding putrefying meat bones to be used as fertiliser and operating a wringing machine in the wash-house. He was shown no compassion because of his one arm, and was strip-searched four times a day as well as enduring regular harassment from some wardens. His diet was poor in both quantity and quality and on a number of occasions he found cockroaches in his food. However, he did find a friendly warden who smuggled out a number of letters that described his experiences in prison, and they were published in some newspapers. Though a political prisoner, Michael Davitt always believed that he was treated worse than ordinary criminals and was allowed no visitors.[37] The ordeal he endured in Dartmoor prison was horrific and, on his release, he made every effort to have the system reformed. His experiences were no different to those of other Fenian prisoners at that time.

Father's Death

Of all that he endured in prison, his most depressing experience was when he learned of his father's death in December 1871, at the age of about fifty-seven.[38] In a letter to his mother on 6 January 1872, Michael wrote:

> The sad tidings of my father's death . . . found me entirely unprepared for such a calamity. I find it impossible to describe to you the sorrow . . . with which the news struck me and the feeling of remorse at the thought of being in part the cause of his demise. He would never have quitted England but for me, and might still be alive had I not compelled him to an unwilling exile. Yet I can conscientiously call heaven to witness that I did it fully believing it would be better for him and you all to be among friends and in a land where the country of his birth would be no reproach to him . . . Still, his dying calls for me will never cease to sound in my ears as so many reproaches for my absence at the last moments of his life. He believed that no one else loved him as I did; but what must have been his thoughts of me when I was not present to comfort him at his last hour? I pray God he did not then upbraid me for my absence. You tell me that he died peacefully, but you omitted to mention whether he left this world fortified with the consolations of religion or not. May God give eternal rest to his soul.[39]

11. *The Padden family grave in the Cathedral Cemetery, Scranton, where Martin Davitt was buried in December 1871. (In addition to Michael's father, his sister Mary (d.1905) and brother-in-law, Neil Padden (d.1882), were later buried in the same plot).*

The letter shows the great love and respect he had for his father. Martin was buried in plot number 24, section D1, at the Cathedral Cemetery, Oram Boulevard, Scranton, Pennsylvania.[40] In 1873, Catherine Davitt and two of her daughters, Anne and Sabina, moved from Scranton to Manayunk, a suburb of Philadelphia, in the hope of better employment opportunities.[41] Anne married Edward Crowley, an Irish-American, in St. John the Baptist Church, Manayunk, on 7 October 1877.[42]

Amnesty Campaign and Home Rule

A movement started in 1868 led to the foundation of the Amnesty Association in June 1869, with Isaac Butt as president, to campaign for the release of prisoners who had been sentenced to long periods of penal servitude following the abortive Fenian rising of 1867. Many leading Fenians including Charles Kickham were released in 1869 by the new Liberal government and others like John Devoy and Jeremiah O'Donovan Rossa in 1871. Meetings on behalf of the Amnesty Association led to the inauguration of the Home Rule Association by Isaac Butt on 19 May 1870. Butt (1813-'79), a County Donegal-born barrister, and Member of Parliament for Limerick from 1871, was to lead MPs supporting Home Rule in Westminster from 1873 to 1879. (In the general election of 1868, Irish Members of Parliament had been either Conservatives or Liberals.) Under Butt's leadership, the Home Rule League was founded in November 1873 to seek self-government for Ireland within a federal system in the United Kingdom. In the general election of 1874, the first after the enactment of the Secret Ballot in 1872, sixty professed supporters of Home Rule were elected out of 103 Irish representatives in the House of Commons, but only about a third were formally committed to that objective. The Home Rule League became the first attempt by Irish members to organise a separate party in the House of Commons and evolved into the Irish Party, or as it was more commonly called the Irish Parliamentary Party. Isaac Butt made sure that Michael Davitt was not forgotten and kept up his amnesty campaign for the release of the remaining Fenian prisoners.[43]

Release on Ticket-of-Leave

Eventually, on 19 December 1877, at the age of thirty-one, Michael Davitt was released on a ticket-of-leave in response to the amnesty campaign, after seven years, seven months and five days imprisonment.[44] This ticket-of-leave authorised his release during the remainder of his term of penal servitude on specified conditions: the two most important being that he was not convicted of some indictable offence or that the ticket-of-leave was not revoked by the queen. While the Fenians released under the amnesty in 1871 were granted a free pardon, Michael Davitt and three Fenians released in January 1878 only received remissions of their sentences, which meant that they could be incarcerated without a trial during the remaining period if they breached any condition of their release.

While Davitt was still a Fenian, he had begun to question the rigidity and intolerance of the organisation.[45] He saw the need for far more flexibility in Fenian policy, especially in its attitude to the Parliamentary Party, and deeply appreciated the role played by Members of Parliament in his own early release. Despite what he endured in Dartmoor prison, Michael Davitt never showed any hostility or bitterness to any person, but strongly questioned the punitive role of the system. His health suffered while in prison, and thereafter he was never a robust person. After rejoining the IRB, he was elected to the supreme council as a representative for the north of England. Although unknown in Ireland at the time of his conviction, his prison ordeal was well publicised and, on his release, he was hailed as a national hero, a model of invincible resistance to British rule in Ireland. With spirit unbroken, he had the interest and determination to return to his earlier objectives of working for Irish independence and the replacement of the landlord system.

2

References and Notes

1. Census of Ireland, 1851.
2. Killanin, Lord, and Duignan, Michael V., *The Shell Guide to Ireland*, p. 76.
3. *Ibid.*
4. Moody, T. W., *Davitt and Irish Revolution* 1846-82, pp. 1 and 5 (referred too as Moody hereafter). The actual site of the house is believed to be on the Bellavary side of the friary near the river Straide.
5. Moody, pp. 5, 6 and 7.
6. King, Carla, *Michael Davitt*, p. 11 and Moody, pp. 5 and 6.
7. Moody, p. 5, and Davitt, Michael, in King, Carla (ed.), *Jottings in Solitary*, pp. 3-5.
8. *Ibid.*, p. 6.
9. Davitt, Michael, in King, Carla, (ed.), *Jottings in Solitary*, pp. 3-5.
10. Moody, p. 6.
11. *Ibid.*, pp. 8 and 9.
12. *Ibid.*, p. 9.
13. Moody, pp. 9-11.
14. Moody, pp. 9-11. For an account of the Davitt family in Haslingden, see a pamphlet, Dunleavy, John, *Davitt and Haslingden*.
15. *Defence of the Land League*, p. 202. A plaque at the back of Swinford District Hospital marks the site of one of the best preserved famine graves in the country, where 564 are reported to have been buried. The building facing the main road is the only surviving section of the workhouse.
16. Moody, p.15. (Ewood Mill was about a two mile walk from his home.)
17. *Ibid.*, p. 17.
18. *Ibid.*, p. 18.
19. *Ibid.*, p. 19.
20. *Ibid.*
21. *Ibid.*, pp. 19 and 20.
22. *Ibid.*, p 21. (The building is now the local library.)
23. *Ibid.*, p. 44.
24. *Ibid.*, p. 49.
25. *Ibid.*, p. 52.
26. *Ibid.*, p. 53.
27. *Ibid.*, p. 53.
28. *Ibid.*, p. 69. (An Enfield rifle in Hennigan's Heritage Centre, Killasser, Swinford, Co. Mayo, is said to have been made in Birmingham and sent to Ireland by Michael Davitt in the late 1860s.)
29. *Ibid.*, p. 22.
30. *Ibid.*, p. 79.

31. *Ibid.*
32. *Ibid.*, pp. 59.
33. *Ibid.*, p. 60.
    See also T. W. Moody 'Michael Davitt and the "Pen" letter' in *Irish Historical Studies*, IV, no. 15 (1945) pp. 224-253.
34. *Ibid.*, p. 77.
35. *Ibid.*, chapter III.
    For an edited version of a memoir on the trial prepared by Michael Davitt's son, Judge Cahir Davitt, see, A Supplement in *The Irish Times* on Monday, April 30, 1979 entitled 'A Century of the Land League'.
36. Moody, see chapter V for an account of Michael Davitt's prison experiences, as well as Davitt, Michael, *The Prison Life of Michael Davitt*.
37. *Ibid.*
38. *Ibid.*, p. 167.
39. *Ibid.*
40. Martin Davitt was buried in section D1, plot 24, of Cathedral cemetery, Oram Boulevard, Scranton, Pennsylvania. It is the Padden family plot. The following were buried there:
    Martin Davitt, December 1871
    Michael Padden, October 1876 (father of Cornelius, or Neil as he was called).
    Cornelius Padden, March 16, 1882 (husband of Mary Davitt, Michael's sister).
    Mary (Davitt) Padden, June 5, 1905 (sister of Michael).
    James Padden, January 26, 1923.
    Elizabeth J. Padden, November 18, 1939.
    Sabina Padden, March 25, 1958.
    Margaret Padden, June 2, 1964.
    Source: Fitzgerald, John and Joseph, 'Cathedral Cemetery,' in *Mayo Association Yearbook 1998*, pp. 35-37.
41. Moody, p. 169.
42. Moody, p. 173.
43. Sheehy-Skeffington, F., *Michael Davitt: Revolutionary, Agitator and Labour Leader*, p. 59.
44. Moody, p. 180.
45. *Ibid.*, pp. 180-184.

3

The 'New Departure'

After spending Christmas 1877 in London with John Ryan, a former Fenian friend, Michael Davitt and three other released prisoners arrived in Dublin on Sunday 13 January 1878 to a tumultuous welcome headed by Charles Stewart Parnell, John Ferguson and John Dillon.[1] It was Davitt's second time in Dublin, the first as a four and a half year-old child on his way to England, and he was delighted at the warm reception. One of the three other released prisoners, Charles Heapy McCarthy, died on 15 January, and Davitt was involved in the funeral arrangements, with the body of the deceased laying in state in a room of the Carmelite Church in Clarendon Street, Dublin (the only church which agreed to receive the body because he was a Fenian), and the burial in Glasnevin cemetery.[2] On 15 January 1878, Davitt met James Daly from Castlebar, who invited him to visit County Mayo as his guest.[3] Michael Davitt arrived in County Mayo on Saturday 26 January 1878 by train and was greeted by cheering crowds at Ballyhaunis and Claremorris, where he was met by his cousin, John W. Walsh, and the latter's brother-in-law, John W. Nally, both well-known nationalists from Balla. They brought him to Balla for a short visit before going on to Castlebar. Michael Davitt stayed with James Daly in Castlebar and enjoyed seeing some of the places and meeting many people he had heard his parents speak about in their English home. After visiting his native Straide, and meeting his two uncles and cousins and seeing the site of his home where only an old poplar tree then stood, he travelled around by horse car and spoke to crowds in Castlebar, Balla, Swinford and Ballyhaunis.[4] Davitt was thrilled with the warm welcome received in the county and told his mother in a letter that he was 'received like a prince.'[5] During his week-long tour of Mayo he learned of the great distress among the tenant farmers of the county.

James Daly (1836-1910) was already involved in land agitation in the west of Ireland. A native of Boghadoon, near Lahardane (*alias* Lahardaun) in County Mayo, he was a large farmer, a hotel owner, as well as proprietor and editor of the *Connaught Telegraph* newspaper in Castlebar. A town commissioner and poor law guardian, he was the key person in the tenant-right agitation in Connacht from 1876 and a tireless champion of agrarian reform. He was a constitutional reformer, a moderate, and never a member of the IRB. Under his editorship, the *Connaught Telegraph* became the most important newspaper in the country for articulating the grievances of tenant farmers and social conditions in general in the west of Ireland. Despite his large farming interests, James Daly was also a big supporter of those with smallholdings and a constant critic of the avaricious aspirations of graziers.

12. *James Daly, who was the chief pioneer of the land agitation.*

13. *Matthew Harris, who was an early pioneer of the land agitation.*

Before returning to Dublin, Davitt went from Ballyhaunis to Athlone and then called to see Matthew Harris of Ballinasloe, whom he had known prior to his imprisonment. Matthew Harris (1825-'90), a Young Irelander, Fenian and small building contractor, became a pioneer of the tenant-right agitation as well as starting a Tenants' Defence Association in Ballinasloe in 1876, with help from another local man, Michael Malachy O'Sullivan, a Fenian who had lost his job as a teacher because of his political activities. Matthew Harris's grandfather, Peter Harris, of Monasterevan, County Kildare, was hanged for his role in the 1798 rebellion, and his father, a builder, settled in Athlone, where he worked on the erection of St. Mary's Church. Matthew became a slater in the building trade and settled in Ballinasloe. After joining the Fenian organisation in 1865, he served on the supreme council of the IRB, where he met Michael Davitt. They remained great friends until Harris's death in 1890. Both concluded in January 1878 that the only issue upon which Home Rulers and all shades of Irish nationalism could agree was the land question.[6]

Prison Reform

Michael Davitt then went to England and became involved in a campaign for the release of the remaining Irish political prisoners and in advocating prison reform. In May 1878, he published a pamphlet, *The Prison Life of Michael Davitt*, a harrowing account of his prison experiences. During the following weeks, he spoke at several public meetings in England, Belfast and Dublin. Subsequent to making a written submission, he appeared before the Kimberley Commission that had been appointed on 12 February 1878 to examine the working of the Penal Servitude Acts. After being questioned about all the allegations he had made about the prison system, Davitt insisted that he and other Irish political prisoners were the victims of greater harshness and indignity than ordinary criminals. Most of Davitt's evidence related to his own prison experiences, with recommendations for reform, but he was passionate in his desire to see conditions improved for all prisoners, with a system designed to rehabilitate people rather than to punish them. The Kimberley Commission, which reported on 14 July 1879, accepted many of Davitt's recommendations, the chief one being that prisoners with no previous convictions should form a separate group and be segregated from habitual criminals.[7] From personal experience, Michael Davitt was convinced that one of the greatest evils of the penal servitude system was that first-time offenders were ruined by their association with seasoned criminals.

14. *Michael Davitt in Haslingden after his release from prison.*

First Visit to USA

In the aftermath of the failed Fenian rising in 1867, extreme nationalists in the United States, led by Jerome J. Collins, started a new organisation known as Clan na Gael and its key members were William Carroll, a doctor from Philadelphia, and John Devoy (1842-1928). A County Kildare-born Fenian, Devoy went to the United States following his release from an English jail in 1871 as a result of Isaac's Butt's amnesty campaign; the release was on condition that he lived outside the United Kingdom until his sentence had expired. Working as a journalist in New York and Chicago, Devoy joined Clan na Gael on its formation, becoming its most influential member and turning it into the main Irish-American republican organisation. In 1876, he was the chief organiser of the dramatic rescue of six Fenian prisoners from Fremantle, Australia, using a ship named the Catalpa.

15. *John Devoy.*

On 26 July 1878, Michael Davitt boarded a liner at Queenstown (now Cobh) and went on his first journey to the United States to visit his mother and sisters.[8] On arrival in New York on 4 August, he was met by John Devoy, who accompanied him to Philadelphia, where Davitt's mother and two of his sisters had moved following Martin's death. Michael stayed with his mother at 4139 Main Street, Manayunk, Philadelphia, for three weeks and it was an emotional visit.[9] His mother was living with her daughter, Anne, and her son-in-law as well as her other daughter, Sabina. Davitt then went on an extensive lecture tour that was organised for him by Devoy and the Fenians, making a very big impression on his American audiences. His popularity as a public speaker on this American tour and the media contacts he made there were to entice him into a career of public speaking and journalism. He had discussions with many leading Irish-Americans including Patrick Ford (1837-1913), the Galway-born editor of the *Irish World* in New York and John Boyle O'Reilly (1844-'90), a Fenian and writer who became editor and joint owner of the *Pilot* newspaper in Boston.[10] Both were to become very good friends of Michael Davitt, who, as a journalist, subsequently submitted regular articles to American newspapers, especially to the *Irish World* and the *Pilot*.

The 'New Departure'

In America, John Devoy and Michael Davitt formulated what became known as the 'new departure' in the Fenian policy of refusing to co-operate with constitutionalists on the grounds that force was the only means of pursuing Irish independence.[11] It was now proposed that the Fenians should co-operate on specified conditions with the radical wing of the Home Rule Party led by Charles Stewart Parnell in an united effort for national independence and to address the land question. Devoy explained what he called the 'new departure' as follows in the *New York Herald*:

> The change, it is said by those competent to speak on the subject, will take the shape of a combination between the advocates of physical force and those who believe in constitutional agitation, such as will leave the former free to prepare for active work while, in the meantime, giving a reasonable support to a dignified and manly demand for self government on the part of the constitutionalists.[12]

This proposal did not involve an abandonment of the Fenian objective of an Irish republic by physical force, but it did offer an opportunity for collaboration with parliamentarians.

Michael Davitt arrived back in Dublin on 23 December 1878 after a memorable American visit.[13] He and John Devoy went to Paris in January 1879 to put the 'new departure' to the supreme council of the IRB, but its president (and author of the novel, *Knocknagow*), Charles J. Kickham (1826-'82), refused to consider any change in Fenian policy. The supreme council rejected the proposal and refused to commit the IRB to any agrarian agitation, with only Davitt and Matthew Harris dissenting.[14] It did allow individual Fenians to vote at elections, but not to become Members of Parliament. Michael Davitt and John Devoy later put the 'new departure' proposal to Parnell, and he neither accepted or rejected it. This 'new departure' did not take place, but it was superseded by another when Michael Davitt organised constitutionalists, Fenians in Ireland, members of Clan na Gael in America, as well as all other shades of Irish nationalists to support a campaign for land law reform.

Land Act 1860

The prevailing legal position between landlords and tenants was exemplified in the Landlord and Tenant Law Amendment (Ireland) Act of 1860 (Deasy's Act, so called after its sponsor the attorney-general), which established that an express or implied contract was the basis of the relationship between a landlord and tenant. It accepted the premise that land was the exclusive property of the landlord and that tenants contracted to pay a certain rent for the use of specific land for a defined period. It allowed a landlord to recover a holding at the end of a lease or periodic tenancy. The 1860 Act, which favoured the stronger party, strengthened the procedures for ejectment following the non-payment of rent and on issuing notices to quit. At that time, the law was more concerned with property rights than social justice.

Land System in the 1870s

After the Great Famine, social conditions began to improve in rural areas, with some farmers able to increase the size of their farms so as to create more economic holdings. Better market opportunities for Irish beef in the British market and higher prices stimulated a switch from tillage to livestock production, as well as the consolidation and expansion of farms as the number of smallholdings declined. The average age of marriage rose and emigration continued on a big scale. After 1853, there were evictions for many years, but not on the scale experienced during 'the great clearances'.

By the third quarter of the nineteenth century, almost all the land of Ireland was owned by a small number of large landlords. In 1870, 3,761 landlords owned 81 per cent of all the land, while a total of 267,071 tenants, or 50 per cent, occupied holdings of less than fifteen acres.[15] Most tenant farmers held tenancies from year to year or at-will, 526,539, or 77 per cent, in 1870, with 20,217, or 3 per cent, owner-occupied and 135,392, or 20 per cent, in leasehold.[16] The tenants had little say in the rent requested, and it was an easy process for landlords to evict those who were unable to pay their rents by securing a court judgment and giving the required notice. Tenants had few legal rights and could even be evicted at the whim of landlords. The number of evictions in 1870 was 444, with 2,089 persons affected.[17] Nevertheless, by the late 1870s, some landlords were receiving rents that did not cover their costs and at the same time their tenants were demanding rent reductions. The conditions of agricultural labourers, 666,544 in 1871,[18] improved very little from the Great Famine, with most living in poverty. There was continuous friction between landlords and tenants, tenants and tenants, as well as agricultural labourers, resulting in crimes known as 'agrarian outrages' (and involving anything from writing threatening letters to murder).

Demand for Tenant Right

Irish politicians were slow to take up the land question and, indeed, were slower still to see that the solution could come with the abolition of landlordism. County Laois-born James Fintan Lalor (1807-'49) had raised the issue of undoing the conquest and addressing the land question at the height of the Great Famine in 1847 in a series of letters to the *Nation,* a weekly newspaper founded in October 1842 by Charles Gavin Duffy (1816-1903), Thomas Davis (1814-1845) and John Blake Dillon (1816-1866). He advocated 'the land of Ireland for the people of Ireland' and recommended linking the land and national questions so as to give strength to both, with his proposed weapon a general strike against rent. Lalor's views were promoted in America by a radical nationalist, John Mitchel (1815-'75), following his escape from Van Diemen's Land (Tasmania) in 1853, but they had little influence in Ireland from 1847 to 1879.

After the formation of the Tenant Right League in 1850, the demand was for tenant-right: the protection of tenants rather than making them owners. This was encapsulated by the demand for 'three Fs': fair rent, fixity of tenure and free sale, to be pursued by an independent Irish Party at Westminster. It was intended that a fair rent would be established by an impartial valuation, while fixity of tenure meant undisturbed occupancy once this rent was paid. Free sale was the right of a tenant farmer to sell the occupancy of his holding to the highest bidder subject to the landlord's approval of the buyer; this would enable the seller to receive compensation for any improvements made on the holding. If a landlord wished to evict a tenant for any reason other than non-payment of the agreed rent, he would have to pay compensation for the 'disturbance'. These rights existed in Ulster and for that reason tenant-right was then generally referred to as the 'Ulster Custom.' This was the platform on which George Henry Moore (1811-'70) stood for Mayo in the post-famine years, with the support of other prominent nationalists like Charles Gavan Duffy and John Blake Dillon. Progress appeared possible after the 1852 general election when forty-eight supporters of tenant-right were elected out of a total Irish representation of one hundred and three, but the political opportunism of some in advancing their own careers, together with various rivalries and conflicts, led to the disintegration of the group. Even in 1876, when Isaac Butt presented a land reform bill to the House of Commons, all he sought was tenant-right. This bill had huge popular support in Ireland, and its rejection marked the end of the tenant-right era.

There was now a vacuum developing in Irish politics. The ageing and ill Isaac Butt was being challenged by younger more active men like Charles Stewart Parnell, who was elected to parliament in 1875, and who later refused a request from Davitt to join the IRB.[19] Joseph Gillis Biggar (1828-'90), a wealthy Belfast merchant who was elected a Member of Parliament in 1874, started a policy of obstruction in the House of Commons to draw attention to Irish affairs. Biggar, Parnell and others had scant regard for British parliamentary etiquette and took turns in prolonging debates by lengthy speeches as well as the use of various procedural motions, which led to several marathon sessions and obstruction of business in the House of Commons, until the introduction of new regulations made such activity obsolete.

Start of Tenant-Purchase

Tenant-purchase, the conversion of tenants into occupying-owners, started to be considered as a desirable objective. The English economist, John Stuart Mill (1806-'73), expressed the view that the solution to the Irish Land question was tenant-ownership, and he was quoted regularly during the land agitation.[20] When the Liberal Party came to power in December 1868, the new Prime Minister, William Ewart Gladstone (1809-1898), took a keen interest in Ireland, believing that violence came from grievances that were not addressed through political channels. His first action was to disestablish the Church of Ireland, which had been the official State church since the reformation. Under the Irish Church Disestablishment Act of 1869, the Church of Ireland became self-governing, and its estates were sold to tenant farmers, with the government providing loans to cover most of the purchase price, which were repayable by annual instalments; as a result some 6,000 tenant farmers acquired their rented holdings.[21] This was the first initiative in Ireland by Gladstone's government and it marked the beginning of the end of the entrenched privileged position of the Protestant ascendancy. Gladstone then turned his attention to a reform of landlord and tenant law.

Land Act 1870

The first legislation to address some of the grievances of tenant farmers generally was the Landlord and Tenant (Ireland) Act of 1870. It legalised the 'Ulster Custom', the 'three Fs', wherever these rights already existed. In respect of other tenants, the vast majority, the 1870 Act provided that a tenant could not be evicted if he paid his rent and that an outgoing tenant should be compensated for improvements made to his holding. The intention of the Act was to restrain landlords from evicting tenants unfairly, with evictions for reasons other than non-payment of rents giving rise to compensation for 'disturbance'. A tenant evicted for not paying the rent was entitled to no compensation. As fixing of rents remained the prerogative of the landlords, there was no free bargain; tenants had 'Hobson's choice': pay the rent demanded or face eviction. Their position was analogous to that of the unorganised industrial workers of that time.

The 1870 Land Act also contained what were called the Bright Clauses, named after their proposer, John Bright, a Liberal MP. They provided that tenants who wished to buy their farms could borrow two-thirds of the cost from the State and pay off the loan with interest at five per cent in annuities over thirty-five years.[22] The average price was twenty-three and half years' rent. John Bright believed that tenant purchase was the solution to the Irish land question. The implementation of the Act gave rise to a number of difficulties: the 'Ulster Custom' was very difficult to define in law; tenants with leases of 31 years or more were not entitled to compensation for 'disturbance' if their leases were not renewed and, in particular, very few tenants were able to afford a deposit of a third of the price if they wished to purchase their holdings. A total of 877 tenants purchased their holdings under this Act. Nevertheless, the 1870 Land Act was very important as the precursor of a series of Acts which gave the State the legal power to interfere in the contractual relationship between landlords and tenants.

Tenants' Defence Associations

The potato crop failed in 1877, which caused considerable hardship for many families. Demand for livestock, poultry, and other agricultural products declined because of a recession and prices fell. The egg market, which was the main source of income for women in rural areas at that time, collapsed. During 1878, many tenant farmers in the west of Ireland, especially in County Mayo, were unable to pay their rents and credit limits with local shopkeepers were becoming exhausted, resulting in considerable fear of starvation, famine and eviction. The livelihoods of large tenant farmers, shopkeepers, and others dependent on agricultural incomes were also threatened.

James Daly publicly called for the establishment of a land movement in the west in 1875[23] and the following year a Tenants' Defence Association was formed in Ballinasloe by Matthew Harris. Daly gave it considerable publicity in the *Connaught Telegraph* and supported the formation of a similar association in County Mayo.[24] The Mayo Tenants' Defence Association was established in Castlebar on 26 October 1878, with John James Louden, a Westport barrister and large tenant farmer, as chairman and James

Daly as secretary.[25] After his election as a Member of Parliament (MP) for Mayo in the 1874 by-election, John O'Connor Power had given regular reports to constituents on his performance. James Daly was a regular attender at these meetings, from which the Mayo Tenants' Defence Association emerged. Other Tenants' Defence Associations were established around the country. The only farmers' organisation in the country at the time had been the Central Tenants' Defence Association under the leadership of Andrew J. Kettle (1833-1916), a large farmer from County Dublin, but this body was perceived to be orientated towards the interests of farmers with large holdings.[26]

Conditions Deteriorate

The number of families evicted in the country increased from 406 in 1877 to 834 in 1878[27] and there was high emigration to America, chiefly from the west of Ireland. Conditions deteriorated further the following year, especially in County Mayo. Michael Davitt visited Mayo in February 1879 and toured the county with his cousin, J. W. Walshe from Balla, a commercial traveller. The *Connaught Telegraph*, with its motto, 'be just and fear not', carried stories of the tenants' plight week after week. A succession of bad harvests, falling agricultural prices, bad weather, accumulated debts and general economic depression, with no opportunities for seasonal employment in Britain, had created a general fear of famine. The poverty witnessed by Michael Davitt on his tour of County Mayo had a big effect on him, and he had a deep sympathy for the local agitation underway in the west of Ireland as a spontaneous response to a desperate situation.[28]

Organising the 'New Departure'

Michael Davitt claimed that he came out of prison with the Land League on his mind.[29] From the time of his family's eviction, he disliked the landlord system and wished to see it changed, but initially he had no clear idea as to how that could be achieved. He tells us what he thought of the landlord system in *The Fall of Feudalism in Ireland*:

> They were not only Irish landlords; they were the political garrison of England in Ireland, equipped with every weapon and resource at the disposal of a great empire for their protection. They could influence the imperial Parliament for all the coercion their injustice needed as a compelling power to the attainment of their desires. They were a class who had, by aid of this empire, seized all the spoils of conquest – land, government, law, authority, patronage, and wealth – and were backed in their secure possession by all the latent prejudices of anti-Celtic feeling in the English mind.
>
> The contest for the recovery of the soil of Ireland was waged, therefore, against all the internal agencies and external forces of this buttressed, feudal garrison. It was always England's soldiers, England's laws, or England's judges that confronted the tenants, cottiers, or labourers of the land whenever, singly or in combination, they had to assert the ordinary claims of humanity, in illegal or other ways, against this despotic social and political ruling power.
>
> Neither law nor land, homes or government, belonged to the people. They were treated as intruders and outlaws in their fatherland.[30]

Early in 1879, Davitt saw the potential of the land agitation underway in the west of

Ireland to combine the land and national issues for a major assault on the landlord system by merging the energies of constitutional nationalists, revolutionary nationalists and those interested in agrarian reform. His views were beginning to change from reforming the landlord-tenant relationship to abolishing the system and turning the occupying tenants into owners.

The agrarian crisis of 1879 provided a justification for a radical reform of the landlord system, and Michael Davitt became the organiser and inspiration behind a movement which, supported by finance from America and elsewhere, merged constitutionalists and Fenians, tenant farmers, large and small, agricultural labourers as well as towns-people into a war of 'aggressive moral force' with the immediate aim of resisting evictions and the ultimate objective of abolishing the landlord system. Each major participant group had its own agenda. The Fenians believed that a British parliament of landlords would make very few concessions to tenant farmers in Ireland and this could precipitate some Irish MPs withdrawing from the House of Commons. The constitutionalists wanted popular support. While Michael Davitt also sought Irish independence, the land question had moved to the top of his agenda, and he became the catalyst to bring these disparate shades of Irish nationalism together. The 'new departure' was about to take effect.

3

References and Notes

1. Moody, p. 188.
2. *Ibid.*, pp. 189-190.
3. Moody, p. 190.
4. *Ibid.*, pp. 190-198.
5. *Ibid.*, p. 193.
6. Egan, Rev. Patrick K., *The Parish of Ballinasloe – Its History from the Earliest times to the present century*, pp. 267, 274 and 277.
7. Moody, pp. 218-220.
8. *Ibid.*, p. 221.
9. *Ibid.*, p. 226.
10. *Ibid.*, chapter VII.
11. *Ibid.*
12. 27 October 1878, quoted in Moody (p. 251) and Lyons, F.S.L., *Charles Stewart Parnell*, p. 81.
13. Moody, p. 268.
14. *Ibid.*, pp. 277-282.
15. *Ibid.*, p. 29 and appendices A and B.
16. *Ibid.*, p.30.
17. *Ibid.*, appendix D, p. 563.
18. *Ibid.*, appendix C, p.561.
19. Lyons, F.S.L., *Charles Stewart Parnell*, p. 78.
20. Moody, pp. 37-38.
21. Lyons, F.S.L., *Ireland Since the Famine*, pp. 144-145.
22. *Ibid.*, pp. 144-146.
23. Clark, Samuel, *Social Origins of the Irish Land War*, p. 273.
24. Jordan, Jr., Donald, *Land and Popular Politics in Ireland, County Mayo from the Plantation to the Land War*, pp. 209-210.
25. Moody, p. 271.

26.   *Ibid.*, p. 273.
27.   *Ibid.*, appendix D.
28.   *Ibid.*, p. 283.
29.   *Defence of the Land League*, p. 2.
30.   p. xvii.

4

The Land League

The next stage of the land agitation started at Irishtown, County Mayo, in April 1879. Walter Joseph Bourke, an absentee landlord in the Irishtown area, died in 1873, with the estate passing to his son, Joseph, an army surgeon stationed in Hampshire, who was a nephew of Canon Geoffrey Bourke, parish priest of Kilvine, the local parish.[1] Some tenants on the estate were under threat of eviction in January 1879, but T. W. Moody wrote: 'responsibility for the harsh treatment of these tenants may well have been that of the absentee owner, Joseph Bourke, not that of his resident uncle, the canon'[2]. Canon Bourke later supported the Land League. The tenants of the Bourke estate in Irishtown met James Daly, as editor of the *Connaught Telegraph*, in January 1879 and asked him to publish their grievances. He rejected their request, in fear of libel action, but advised them to hold a public meeting to ventilate tenant grievances in general, as well as demanding a reduction in their rents.[3] A meeting was held in February 1879 in Claremorris attended by James Daly, Michael Davitt, John O'Kane, J. W. Walshe, J. P. Quinn and P. W. Nally, at which arrangements were made for a demonstration to be held at Irishtown on Sunday 20 April 1879. With the exception of James Daly, the other chief organisers of the Irishtown meeting were Fenians: John O'Kane, the head of the IRB in Mayo, John W. Walshe, from Balla, a cousin of Michael Davitt, J. P. Quinn, a local school-teacher, and Patrick W. Nally, from Balla, a farmer and an outstanding athlete. Michael Davitt undertook to engage the speakers and draft resolutions for the meeting.[4] The platform was erected on the land of Mrs. Higgins by Jimmy Daly (Crimlin), Michael Cullinan (Drymills), Patrick Corr, John Corr, Jimmy Rattigan, Pat Ronayne, Andy Mullarkey and J. Leonard, and it was guarded the night before the historic meeting by Pat Ruane, Thomas Daly and John Bourke. The timber for the platform was loaned by Joe Dalton of McDonnell's store in Milltown on condition that no nails were put in it.[5] The meeting was announced in the *Connaught Telegraph* on 22 February and notices were displayed around the district.

The Irishtown meeting was chaired by James Daly (Castlebar) and the speakers were Thomas Brennan (Dublin), John O'Connor Power, MP for Mayo, John Ferguson, Glasgow, John James Louden, from Westport, Matthew Harris and Michael Malachy O'Sullivan from Ballinasloe. Michael Davitt did not attend the meeting, presumably because he was a convict on a ticket-of-leave and did not wish to cause any controversy that might affect the meeting. Thomas Brennan (1854-1915), a native of Slane, County Meath, was a Fenian and a clerk in the North Dublin City Milling Company's establishment in Castlebar, and later in the company's office in Dublin. John O'Connor Power (1846-1919), from Ballinasloe, Co. Galway, spent some time in Lancashire as a young man where he knew Michael Davitt and became a Fenian organiser. He turned to constitutional politics and in 1874 was elected as a Member of Parliament for Mayo. He was the only MP at the Irishtown meeting. John Ferguson (1836-1906) was a Belfast-born Presbyterian who moved to Glasgow and became involved in a stationery and printing business there. He was a big supporter of Isaac Butt's Home Rule initiative. All the speakers at the Irishtown meeting had a Fenian involvement except for James Daly, John James Louden and John Ferguson.

Three resolutions were put to the Irishtown meeting and carried; the first and second were written by Michael Davitt and the third was drafted locally.[6] The resolutions were as follows:

1. Whereas, the social condition of the Irish people having been reduced, through their subjection to England and its coercive legislation, to a state below that of any civilised country in the world; and whereas, the mouth-piece of English public opinion when speaking of continental mis-government in late years having declared that 'government should be for the good of the governed, and that whatever rulers will fully and persistently postpone the good of their subjects either in the interests of foreign states, or to assist theories of religion or politics, such rulers have thereby forfeited all claim to allegiance'; be it therefore resolved, that we Irishmen assembled to-day in our thousands do hereby endorse the foregoing declarations as embodying the position and wrongs of our misgoverned and impoverished country, and as likewise affording us a justification for recording our unceasing determination to resort to every lawful means whereby our inalienable rights – political and social – can be regained from our enemies.

2. That as the land of Ireland, like that of every other country, was intended by a just and all-providing God for the use and sustenance of those of His people to whom he gave inclination and energies to cultivate and improve it, any system which sanctions its monopoly by a privileged class, or assigns its ownership and control to a landlord caste, to be used as an instrument of usurious or political self-seeking, demands from every aggrieved Irishman an undying hostility, being flagrantly opposed to the first principle of their humanity – self preservation.

3. A resolution demanding a reduction in unjust rents by local and Mayo landlords.[7]

The meeting, which was attended by a crowd variously stated to be from 4,000 to 13,000, was most successful: the eviction notices were withdrawn from the Bourke tenants and the rent was reduced by twenty-five per cent. The Irishtown meeting ignited the flame that was to change the face of rural Ireland, and this small Mayo village became 'the cradle of the Land League'. This was soon evident when a big meeting was held at Knock, County Mayo, on Sunday 1 June 1879 to protest against the language used by the local parish priest the previous Sunday when criticising the organisers of the Irishtown meeting, especially John O'Kane of Claremorris, the IRB organiser in Mayo.

Charles Stewart Parnell

Prior to the Irishtown meeting, Michael Davitt asked Charles Stewart Parnell to lead a national movement in support of tenant farmers at a meeting in Dublin on 6 April 1879 attended by John Devoy.[8] He first met Parnell in London a few days after his release from prison in December 1877 and was very impressed by him. His first opinion on Parnell as recorded in *The Fall of Feudalism in Ireland* (1904) was: 'An Englishman of the strongest type, moulded for an Irish purpose'.[9]

Parnell was born on 27 June 1846 (the same year as Michael Davitt) into a Protestant landlord family in Avondale, near the beautiful Vale of Avoca, in County Wicklow. His mother, Delia Stewart, was an American with strong anti-English sentiments, while his paternal ancestors had opposed the Act of Union in 1800 and supported Catholic Emancipation. After attending the University of Cambridge and inheriting the family's 1,893-hectare estate, he was elected an MP for Meath at a by-election in April 1875. An early supporter of the obstructionist tactics of Joseph Biggar in the House of Commons, he was seen in 1879 as a future leader of the Irish Party at Westminister. Michael Davitt, conscious of his own strengths and weaknesses, showed great vision, judgment, courage, and, indeed, humility in his invitation to Parnell. Admiring his commanding presence, Davitt believed that Parnell would bring considerable prestige to the land movement. If Parnell was to achieve his ambition and become a national leader, it was important for him to have popular support in Ireland. A national land movement, with the 'new departure' in Fenian policy, offered a great opportunity, but he was reluctant to commit himself in case it got out of control. Even though he was a landlord, he had no difficulty with tenant-ownership as the solution to the Irish land question. Davitt, Devoy and Parnell met again on 1 June 1879, when social conditions in the west were deteriorating. After the successful Irishtown meeting, Davitt and Devoy assured Parnell that individual Fenians could participate in agrarian agitation so long as it was not incompatible with their ideals, and that a large number would support his leadership on certain conditions, including that the solution of the land question was to be tenant proprietorship, achieved by compulsory puchase.[10] Parnell still refused to accept Davitt's invitation, but agreed to honour a promise he made to speak at a meeting planned for Westport, the seat of the Marquis of Sligo, a landlord with the largest estate in County Mayo.

Westport and other Meetings

The next milestone-event in the land agitation occurred again in County Mayo, when, on 8 June 1879, Charles Stewart Parnell attended and spoke at a public meeting in Westport, despite ecclesiastical objections, especially from the eighty-nine year old archbishop of Tuam, John MacHale. A letter was published in the *Freeman's Journal* on 7 June, under the name of Archbishop MacHale, criticising the land meeting to be held in Westport.[11] (It is difficult to accept that a fully alert Archbishop John McHale would have opposed the land agitation and it is now generally believed that the letter was written by Dr Thomas MacHale, the archbishop's nephew.) Michael Davitt described the letter as 'this bolt from the blue'[12] and admired Parnell's courage in fulfilling the engagement. He wrote in *The Fall of Feudalism in Ireland*:

> Here was a leader at last who feared no man who stood against the people, no matter what his reputation of record might be; a leader, too, who, though a Protestant, might, on that account, be more politically subservient to a great Catholic prelate on public issues than the Catholic nationalists of Mayo would consent to be in such a democratic cause. It was Mr. Parnell's first momentous step in his progress towards

the leadership of a race mostly Catholic, and I have always considered it the most courageously wise act of his whole political career.[13]

Michael Davitt spoke at the Westport meeting, his first speech to an Irish audience on the land question, stating that he was an unrepentant separatist and that the land problem had its origin in the conquest of Ireland. After advising the audience 'to keep a firm grip on your homesteads,' Charles Stewart Parnell supported a 'fair rent' depending on the circumstances of the time until a final settlement of the land question could be achieved by tenant-ownership. The meeting, which was chaired by James Daly, was widely reported in both English and Irish newspapers, in contrast to the Irishtown meeting that was virtually ignored, except for the *Connaught Telegraph* and *Tuam Herald*. Both of these newspapers gave extensive coverage to the campaign for radical land reform.

The Westport meeting, at which the slogan 'the land for the people' was first used, became the most important of the entire land agitation. (A monument was erected at the site of the Davitt/Parnell Westport meeting at Attyreece, Westport, by the Westport Historical Society in 1979.) Subsequently, further meetings were held in Milltown, Co. Galway, and at Claremorris, Balla, and Shrule in County Mayo, all of which were attended by Michael Davitt.[14] John Dillon (1851-1927) and Canon Ulick Bourke (1829-1887) joined the land agitation at the Claremorris meeting, and both became good friends and supporters of Michael Davitt.[15] John Dillon, the second son of the Ballaghadereen-born Young Ireland leader, John Blake Dillon, qualified as a doctor, but never practised. A strong nationalist and sharing Michael Davitt's views on the landlord system, he was a welcome recruit to the land campaign. Despite some ecclesiastical opposition, the agitation, which had no clerical involvement at the start, was publicly supported by many priests and some bishops, especially Archbishop Thomas William Croke of Cashel (after whom Croke Park is named), who became a life-long friend of Michael Davitt, as well as Dr Francis Mac Cormack, bishop of Achonry, and Dr Patrick Duggan, bishop of Clonfert. The main issues raised in the speeches at the Westport and later meetings were Ireland's right to self-government, the abolition of the landlord system, converting the occupiers into owners, protecting tenants against eviction, helping those evicted and calling for a reduction in rents.

'National Land League of Mayo'

By August 1879, Parnell was still unable to give a commitment that he would lead a national land movement. Consequently, Michael Davitt decided to press ahead and start a movement in County Mayo that could later evolve into a national body. He called a convention for the establishment of a league of tenant farmers in County Mayo, and an organisation known as 'The National Land League of Mayo' was inaugurated on Saturday 16 August 1879 in James Daly's Hotel, Castlebar (now the Imperial Hotel).[16] The constitution and rules were written and proposed by Michael Davitt. The meeting was chaired by John J. Louden, who was elected president, with James Daly vice-president, P. W. Nally[17] and J. W. Walshe as secretaries, but Nally, who was not in attendance, later declined to act.[18] The objectives of the 'National Land League of Mayo' were as follows:

1. To watch over the interests of the people it represents, and protect the same as far as may be in its power to do so from an unjust or capricious exercise of power or privilege on the part of landlords or any other class in the community.

2. To resort to every means compatible with justice, morality, and right reason which shall not clash defiantly with the constitution upheld by the powers of the British Empire in this country for the abolition of the present land laws of Ireland, and the substitution in their place of such a system as shall be in accord with the social rights and interests of our people, the traditions and moral sentiments of our race, and which the contentment and prosperity of our country imperiously demand.

3. Pending a final satisfactory settlement of the land question, the duty of this body will be to expose the injustice, wrong, or injury which may be inflicted upon any farmer in Mayo, either by rack-renting, eviction, or other arbitrary exercise of power which the existing laws enable the landlords to exercise over their tenantry, by giving all such arbitrary acts the widest publicity, and meeting their perpetration with all the opposition which the laws for the preservation of the peace will permit.

16. *Patrick J Nally from Balla, one of the organisers of the Irishtown land protest meeting, was elected secretary of the 'National Land League of Mayo'. He later influenced Michael Cusack to establish the Gaelic Athletic Association.*

In furtherance of which the following plan will be adopted:

Returns to be obtained, printed, and circulated of the number of landlords in this county, the amount of acreage in possession of same, and the means by which such lands were obtained, the farms owned by each, with the conditions under which they are held by their tenants, and the excess of rent paid by same over the government valuation. To publish by placard, or otherwise, notice of contemplated evictions for non-payment of exorbitant rent, or other unjust cause, and the convening of public meetings if necessary or expedient, as near the scene of such evictions as circumstances will allow, and on the day fixed upon for the same. The publication of a list of evictions carried out, together with cases of rack-renting, giving full particulars of same, name of landlord, agents, etc., concerned, and the number of people evicted by such acts. The publication of the names of all persons who shall rent or occupy land or farms from which others have been dispossessed for non-payment of exorbitant rents, or who shall offer a higher rent for land or farms than that paid by the previous occupier.

4. This body to undertake the defence of such of its members or others of local clubs affiliated with it who may be required to resist by law actions of landlords or their agents, who may purpose doing them injury, wrong, or injustice in connection with their land or farms.

5. To render assistance when possible to such farmer members as may be evicted or otherwise wronged by the landlords or their agents.

6. To undertake the organising of local clubs or defence associations in the baronies, towns, and parishes of this county, the holding of public meetings and demonstrations on the land question, and the printing of pamphlets on that

and other subjects for the information of the farming-classes.

7.   Finally, to act as a vigilance committee in Mayo, noting the conduct of its grand jury, poor-law guardians, town commissioners, and members of Parliament, and pronouncing on the manner in which their respective duties are performed, whenever the interests, social or political, of the people represented by this club render it expedient to do so.[19]

These objectives charted a plan of action, with the second one interpreted as a demand for tenant-ownership, which was then a really radical proposal. As Members of Parliament were not paid for their services at that time, they were almost all landowners, and obviously they would not easily consider a proposal for tenant-ownership of the land, but the campaign was underway. As to be expected, the demand for tenant-ownership gained popular support among the tenant farmers. Pending the attainment of tenant proprietorship, it was agreed to publicise injustices, to protect tenants from evictions, to organise public demonstrations at eviction scenes as well as helping those who were evicted. The motto was: 'The land of Ireland belongs to the people of Ireland'.

According to Michael Davitt, the 'National Land League of Mayo' was part of his strategy to establish a national organisation 'for the control and direction of the new movement' that would 'supplant the tenants' defence associations' with 'an aggressive movement which would try to rally the whole country in the fight against the whole land system.' He also envisaged the development of 'root principles' for the land agitation and in particular that the 'National Land League of Mayo' would be 'the nucleus for a national body' which would induce Charles Stewart Parnell to lead the movement.[20] In fact, the 'National Land League of Mayo' only met once,[21] but it did fulfil the role envisaged by Davitt. The formation of the 'National Land League of Mayo' took the initiative away from the local organisers in the county led by James Daly and focused the land agitation towards a national movement.[22]

Later land meetings were held during 1879 in Tuam, Newport, Killala, Aughamore, and Annaghdown, with Michael Davitt the main speaker at each, and the agitation spread to several other counties. Davitt's leadership and indefatigable work-rate in agitating for a change in the landlord system kept morale high in the west of Ireland, while he endeavoured to broaden the support base of the movement on a national scale.

Irish National Land League

In September 1879, Charles Stewart Parnell finally agreed to lead a national land movement. He agreed to incorporate the Central Tenants' Defence Association into the new body and to convene the inaugural meeting for the Imperial Hotel in Sackville Street (now O'Connell Street), Dublin, with an 'appeal to the Irish race' written by Michael Davitt inviting selected people to join.[23] Davitt also wrote guidance notes for local branches. Andrew J. Kettle, secretary of the Central Tenants' Defence Association, who had become a close friend of Parnell, chaired the inaugural meeting, held on 21 October 1879.[24] The Mayo Land League lasted two months and was then absorbed into the Irish National Land League, with Charles Stewart Parnell as president and Michael Davitt one of its secretaries. The objectives of the Irish National Land League were to achieve a reduction in rack-rents and 'to facilitate the obtaining of the ownership of the

*17. Charles Stewart Parnell,
President of the Irish National
Land League.*

soil by the occupiers'. These were to be attained by promoting organisation among the tenant farmers and by defending those threatened with eviction for refusing to pay unjust rents.'[25] The objectives of the Irish National Land League were less radical than the Mayo organisation it replaced, but they were deemed by Parnell to be reasonable and practical proposals that could be promoted through political channels in the House of Commons.

The National Land League had an executive of seven and a overall committee of fifty-four. The executive consisted of Charles Stewart Parnell, three secretaries, Michael Davitt, Thomas Brennan, who had spoken at the Irishtown meeting, and Andrew J. Kettle, together with three treasurers, Patrick Egan, Joseph Biggar, MP, and William Henry O'Sullivan, MP. Kettle was the only farmer on the executive, but the three influential people were Michael Davitt, Thomas Brennan and Patrick Egan, all honorary part-time officials.[26] This triumvirate conducted the daily business of the Land League, with Davitt responsible for organisation, Brennan for propaganda, and Egan for finance.[27] Patrick Egan (1841-1919), a native of Ballymahon, County Longford, was a wealthy businessman, co-owner, with James Rourke, of the City Bakery, and managing-director of the North Dublin City Milling Company. A former member of the supreme council of the IRB and now an active supporter of Home Rule, he was widely respected for his integrity, sagacity, prudence and management skills. Other members of the Land League Committee included early supporters of the cause such as James Daly, John Dillon, John Ferguson, Matthew Harris, John J. Louden, John O'Connor Power, MP, and James Rourke, who became a very close friend of Michael Davitt's.

Branches of the Land League were formed in almost every parish in the country (outside parts of Ulster where the Ulster Custom prevailed), and Michael Davitt addressed the inaugural meetings of several branches weekly. The Land League, which made only a limited impact in Ulster, was not a homogeneous organisation; its membership consisted of large tenant farmers, subsistence tenant farmers, graziers, agricultural labourers and the urban middle class. While the campaign was initiated because many tenant farmers with smallholdings were unable to pay their rents, most large tenant farmers and graziers were well able to meet their obligations but, in depressed times, they believed that rents should be reduced accordingly and also saw a possible opportunity to obtain ownership of their holdings. As the land agitation spread into the east and south of Ireland, farmers with larger farms were able to secure control of the local Land League branches and later to direct the policy of the central executive to serve their interests, rather than those of farmers with smallholdings who initiated the campaign. There was also continuing conflict between agricultural labourers and farmers. While Davitt was always aware of these class tensions within the Land League, his primary objective at that stage was to see the end of the landlord system. As the key personality on the Land League executive, the period from October 1879 to May 1880 was hectic for him, with meetings, speeches, organisation, interminable correspondence, maintaining the unity and focus of the organisation, reports to friends in America, articles to American newspapers, and the distribution of relief money to families in need. Davitt earned some income from his journalistic work with American newspapers, especially the *Pilot* and the *Irish World*.

Gurteen meeting

The government came under pressure to take action against the Land League and its leaders. On 19 November 1879, Michael Davitt was arrested for an alleged seditious speech on 2 November at Gurteen, County Sligo, during the first Land League meeting in that county. Two other speakers were also charged, James Daly from Castlebar and James Bryce Killen from Belfast. The trial, which began in Sligo on Monday 24 November, became a farce and Michael Davitt described the scene thus:

> The day's proceedings began by the Sligo brass band and a huge crowd escorting the prisoners from the county jail to the trial, the procession parading the whole town on its way to the court, like a newly arrived circus company. The court was as crowded as a theatre with the attraction of a popular play, a large number of ladies being present. Then began the solemn farce of reading an indictment and the customary legal fray over points, precedents and previous judgments between the opposing counsel . . . In this manner the first session of the magisterial investigation went on and ended, the sitting being adjourned until the following morning. Back we went to prison, the brass band leading, the police escorting, and the whole town following and cheering Parnell, Dillon and the prisoners. And when the 'villains' of the peace were disposed of for the night in the jail, a public meeting was held in the town, addressed by Mr. Parnell and others in speeches that rang with fierce denunciations of the prosecution, and the curtain was rung down upon the first act of the precious performance.[28]

James Daly, defended by John J. Louden, was the first to be tried and he was released on bail. Davitt defended himself and, after being committed for trial, was released on bail. The trial of Killen was dramatic, with John Rea, a Belfast Protestant engaged by Joseph Biggar, defending. Rea insisted on addressing the presiding magistrate as 'Mr. Promoted-Policeman', as he had formerly been a member of the constabulary and when the magistrate mispronounced a word, Rea was on his feet demanding to know 'whether it was permissible for a man in the pay of the crown to murder the Queen's English?[29] The hearings were widely covered by newspapers in Ireland, England and America, generating considerable favourable press coverage for the Land League. The charges against all defendants were later dropped.

Meanwhile, Fr. Denis O'Hara (1850-1922), a native of Cloonacool, Co. Sligo, who became parish priest of Killedan (Kiltimagh) in 1887, spoke at the Gurteen meeting and thereafter was a very close friend of Michael Davitt. Davitt tells us in *The Fall of Feudalism in Ireland* what he thought of this County Sligo priest:

> Father Denis O'Hara spoke at the Gurteen meeting and began there a career of work for the good of the people, which has never been surpassed, if ever equalled by any priest who has laboured with the kindest of Irish hearts and the most level of Irish heads, for the protection and the material welfare of the Connaught peasantry.[30]

Straide Meeting

Land League bands were established in many towns and parishes in the west of Ireland. A large number of these bands were in Straide on 1 February 1880 at a huge meeting to hear Michael Davitt speak from a platform erected over the site of the house where he was born. Concluding an emotive speech on that occasion, he said:

> It is no little consolation to know, however, that we are here to-day doing battle against a doomed monopoly, and that the power which has so long domineered over Ireland and its people is brought to its knees at last, and on the point of being crushed forever, and if I am standing to-day upon a platform erected over the ruins of my levelled home, I may yet have the satisfaction of trampling on the ruins of Irish landlordism.[31]

America

Charles Stewart Parnell and John Dillon undertook a very successful tour of America early in 1880 raising funds for the Land League and for the relief of distress in the west. On 2 February 1880, Parnell addressed the House of Representatives in Washington DC and received a great reception. With the support of Michael Davitt, Charles Stewart Parnell was elected an MP for Mayo in the April 1880 general election, but opted for Cork City where he was also elected. Parnell used his growing popularity in the Land League to revitalise the Irish Parliamentary Party and in May 1880 became its leader. The twin strategies of the Land League were vibrant representation in parliament and non-violent mass agitation in Ireland. It was also decided that Michael Davitt should go to the United States to oversee the establishment of an American Land League.

After arriving in New York on 18 May 1880, Michael Davitt was elected as secretary of 'The Irish National Land and Industrial League of the United States' the following day at Trenor Hall.[32] Agreeing to act in that capacity while in the USA, he was then secretary of the Land Leagues on both sides of the Atlantic and in the words of T. W. Moody, 'was received by Irish-Americans as second only to Parnell in the leadership of the Irish nation'.[33] Over the following six months, he built up a central office in New York, addressed meetings all over the United States, from the Atlantic to the Pacific, and raised considerable funds, which were sent direct to Dublin.

Having visited his mother three times since his arrival in the USA in May, Michael Davitt was fortunate to be there when she died at Manayunk, Philadelphia, on 18 July 1880.[34] Her death caused him great remorse and he reflected on how little he had been able to do for her and all the worry his life had caused her. It was her wish to be buried in Turlough, County Mayo, but Michael and his sisters could not afford the expense involved and, to his grief, she was buried on 21 July in the grounds of the Church of Saint John the Baptist, 146 Rector Street, Manayunk.[35] After his mother's interment, Michael Davitt continued his US tour and in September 1880 reached Oakland on the eastern side of San Francisco Bay in California. There, he met a young woman, Mary Jane Yore, an Irish-American, who was to become his wife six years later.[36]

On 8 November 1880, Davitt was a guest at a public meeting organised by a new body, the Ladies' Land League of the United States, in the Cooper Institute, New York. It was founded on 15 October 1880 by Fanny Parnell (1849-1882), a sister of Charles Stewart, and by Ellen Ford, a sister of Patrick Ford, to raise funds for the Irish Land

League.[37] Michael Davitt arrived back in Dublin on 20 November after a very successful US tour, which raised the Irish land question on to a new plane in the United States and generated enormous goodwill and financial support for its reform. He immediately became involved in the Land League work from its office at 39 Upper Sackville Street, Dublin. The following few weeks were very demanding as the land war reached its height.

18. *Catherine Davitt's gravestone in the grounds of the Church of Saint John the Baptist, Manayunk, Philadelphia. There is a harp intertwined with shamrock at the top left and a bunch of shamrock on the top right.*

4

References and Notes

1. Davitt, Michael, *The Fall of Feudalism in Ireland*, pp. 146-7, 150-1.
    Moody, pp. 292-295.
2. Moody, p. 295.
3. *Ibid.*, pp. 284-285.
4. Davitt, Michael, *The Fall of Feudalism in Ireland*, pp. 146-7.

5   Leamy, P.W., 'The Story of Michael Davitt', *Mayo News*, 1946.
     Note: Several six-inch nails had to be inserted in the timber for the erection of the platform. The locals could not afford to pay for the timber, but they decided to keep it and make a few dressers which were sold locally to raise the required money.
     Source: Dr Gay Corr, Galway, whose great great-grandfather and great-granduncle were involved in the erection of the platform.
6.   Moody, p. 291.
7.   Davitt, Michael, *The Fall of Feudalism in Ireland*, p. 148.
8.   Moody, p. 288.
9.   Davitt, Michael, *The Fall of Feudalism in Ireland*, p. 110.
10. Moody, pp. 297-298.
11. Davitt, Michael, *The Fall of Feudalism in Ireland*, p. 153.
     The letter was dated 5 June 1879.
12. *Ibid.*
13. *Ibid.*, pp. 153-154.
14. Moody, p. 306.
15   *Ibid.*, pp. 309-310.
16. *Ibid.*, p. 317.
17. Patrick W. Nally (1856-1891) was a Fenian and a brilliant athlete, who became very interested in forming a national athletics body. Nally organised two national athletic meetings in Balla under the patronage of Charles Stewart Parnell, with the support of the Land League, in opposition to a sports organised by a local landlord. He met Michael Cusack (1847-1906) in 1881 and they discussed the control of athletics in Ireland, the exclusion of labourers from participation, as well as the possibility of establishing an Irish organisation with full autonomy, which *inter alia* led to the establishment of the Gaelic Athletic Association in 1884. However, Nally was not present at the inaugural meeting, as he had been sentenced to ten years' penal servitude for his Fenian activities. He died in Mountjoy Jail on 9 November 1891 and was buried in Glasnevin Cemetery. The Nally Stand in Croke Park was named in his honour from 1954 to 2003, when it was removed as part of the new development.
18. Davitt, Michael, *Defence of the Land League*, p. 225.
19. Davitt, Michael, *The Fall of Feudalism in Ireland*, pp. 162-163.
20. Davitt, Michael, *The Fall of Feudalism in Ireland*, pp. 159-164.
     Jordan Jr., Donald E., *Land and Popular Politics in Ireland: County Mayo from the Plantation to the Land War*, p. 244.
21. Jordan Jr., Donald E., *op.cit.*, p. 244.
22. Lee, Joseph, *The Modernisation of Irish Society*, p. 78.
23. Moody, p. 383.
24. Moody, p. 335.
25   *Ibid.*, p. 335 and Davitt, Michael, *The Fall of Feudalism in Ireland*, p. 172.
26. Moody, pp. 335-344.
27. *Ibid.*, p. 344.
28. *The Fall of Feudalism in Ireland*, p. 183.
29. *Connaught Telegraph*, 29 November and 6 December 1879.
30. *The Fall of Feudalism in Ireland*, p.192.
31. Davitt, Michael, *The Fall of Feudalism in Ireland*, p. 223.
     Note: This meeting became part of the oral history of the county, especially for those whose ancestors were in Straide on that historic occasion and if they were members of any of the Land League bands.
32. Moody, p. 383.
33. *Ibid.*
34. *Ibid.*, p. 396.
35. *Ibid.*, p. 397 (She was buried beside the footpath on the left side of the main entrance).
36. *Ibid.*, p. 407.
37. *Ibid.*, p. 414.

5

The Land War

The land war was a mass movement of agrarian protest and organised passive resistance, initiated and conducted by the Land League from 1879 to 1882. Exploiting the moral power of mass solidarity based on social justice, the Land League's strategy was put into effect long before Mahatma Gandhi preached the doctrine of non-violent resistance to the people of India. Its rhetoric questioned the legitimacy of the landlord ascendancy class in Ireland, as well as the economic and social consequences of the system. With the crisis in agricultural incomes in 1879, many tenant farmers were unable to pay their rents, and when reductions in rent were refused, the Land League led a campaign against the landlords in general. There were numerous mass meetings, with speeches dealing with the conquest of Ireland, the perceived terrible consequences of the imposed landlord system and advice on the proposed collective response. The general *modus operandi* of the Land League involved seeking rent reductions and, if refused, offering a landlord a fair rent having regard to the circumstances of the time, and if this was not accepted, tenants were to pay no rent. They were expected to feed their families before paying rent. Evictions became scenes of great demonstrations, persons evicted were supported during and after their ordeals, an embargo was placed on every farm from which people were evicted, persons charged with agrarian crimes were helped, and 'land-grabbers' were ostracised. The Land League developed a practice of opposing ejectments in the courts and a policy of payment at the last moment so as to make evictions difficult for landlords, while endeavouring to ensure as far as possible that tenants did not lose their holdings. This practice became known as 'rent at the point of the bayonet'. It gave rise to legal costs that were generally paid by the Land League. Some intimidation, violence and homicides did take place but, technically, the Land League was a lawful and non-violent organisation. Although Davitt and other Land League leaders did their best to prevent violent activities, the number of agrarian outrages increased from 863 (including eight homicides) in 1879 to 2,585 (including eight homicides) in 1880.[1] The number of families evicted increased from 1,098 in 1879 to 1,893 in 1880 as the landlords retaliated.[2]

The most effective and dreaded weapon of the Land League was ostracisation, a policy recommended by John Dillon, Charles Stewart Parnell, and especially by Michael Davitt in the programmes of the Mayo and National Land Leagues.[3] Parnell, in a speech in Ennis on 19 September 1880, recommended that 'land grabbers' were to be treated as outcasts and isolated from all human and economic contacts with the community.[4] The

19. *Lough Mask House, Ballinrobe, the residence of Captain Boycott from 1873 to 1880.*

most publicised example of ostracisation took place within a week of the Ennis speech at Lough Mask House, near Ballinrobe, in County Mayo.[5] Captain Charles Cunningham Boycott (1832-1897), a former British army officer and later an unsuccessful farmer in Achill, was appointed agent for the Lough Mask House estate in 1873 by Lord Erne, an absentee landlord. Boycott kept increasing the rent for his tenants, as well as dismissing some employees during a wage dispute. After refusing a request from the Land League for reductions in rent, he insisted on full payment, and when the tenants refused to pay, eviction notices were served on eleven families.

The parish priest of Kilmolara, resident in the Neale, Fr. John O'Malley, organised a campaign of ostracisation against Boycott in September 1880. On 23 September 1880, a crowd approached Lough Mask House, forcing all the staff to leave. It was decided that no one would undertake any work for or provide any service to Captain Boycott. The campaign received wide coverage in the Irish and English newspapers, with *The Times* of London calling on the government to invoke constitutional powers. Eventually, men were brought from the Orange Lodges of Cavan and Monaghan to save the harvest for Captain Boycott, guarded by a big force of troops. Some £350 worth of crops were harvested at an estimated cost of £3,500. The expedition from the north received considerable publicity around the world as did the appalling poverty in County Mayo at the time. Father O'Malley and James Redpath, an American journalist who stayed with him during the campaign, gave a new word to the English language, 'boycott.' Captain Boycott left Ireland as a result, but he retained a small estate at Kildarra, about midway between Ballyhaunis and Irishtown; he returned there frequently on holidays up to the time of his death in 1897.[6]

Agrarian Outrages

The threatened famine of 1879 and 1880 did not take place because of the work of various voluntary relief organisations and the supply of food, clothes and finance from America, Britain, Canada, Australia and other parts of the world. The Land League distributed food, clothes and money it had received, especially from America, and many landlords reduced the rents charged. These activities and a good harvest in 1880 averted the expected famine. A big problem still remained; numerous tenant farmers were unable to pay their rents or clear off accumulated arrears, with the landlords demanding payments or else evictions. The response was not the isolated violence of the past, but a continuation of the well-organised collective revolt of the Land League. This was infused with an element of Fenianism as well as the aggressive collective spirit of an industrial dispute, which were new features in agrarian protests.

As agrarian outrages increased during the second half of 1880, the Land League established 'land courts' for the trial of people who violated its code of conduct. The Land League could not accept responsibility for the 'courts,' but they were quite effective in some areas. By the end of 1880, the Land League had destabilised the rural economy and virtually controlled the country, shaking the landlord system to the core, and had a very effective public relations campaign in place. For the first time, the tenant farmers as a class stood up to the landlords and eventually had the system changed.

A Liberal government, led by W. E. Gladstone, came to power in April 1880, with W. E. Forster as Chief Secretary for Ireland. Influenced by Forster, the government became alarmed at the increasing violence in Ireland and was under considerable pressure to take appropriate action. Charles Stewart Parnell and thirteen other Land League members were charged with criminal conspiracy in November 1880, but in January 1881, the jury failed to agree and the defendants were discharged, which led to further criticism by large sections of the British press.[7] Eventually, the government decided on a policy of coercion and concession, the former involved coercion legislation and the latter the Land Act of 1881. Landlords established the Property Defence Association in December 1880 to protect their interests

Coercion

In January 1881, the government introduced the first of two coercion bills, the Protection of Person and Property Bill, to suppress the Land League. It was designed to legalise the arrest and imprisonment without trial of anyone suspected of promoting illegal activities.[8] The Irish Parliamentary Party considered a proposal to withdraw from the House of Commons and establish a national convention in Dublin, as well as launching a 'no rent' strike, but no agreement was reached. Parnell and other Irish MPs opposed the bill and made every effort to obstruct its passage through the House of Commons. Even before the passing of the bill, Michael Davitt's ticket-of-leave (parole) was revoked and he was arrested in Dublin on 3 February 1881.[9] After being brought to Millbank prison in London for two nights, he was transferred to Portland Prison in Dorset, where he was detained for the next fifteen months. On 3 February 1881, Patrick Egan moved to Paris with the Land League records and continued to act as treasurer until October, when the Irish National League was established.[10]

The arrest of Michael Davitt infuriated most of the Irish MPs. John Dillon was the first to protest and was suspended and ejected from the House of Commons, to be followed by Parnell and thirty-four others. There was considerable pressure on Parnell from some Irish MPs not to return, but with characteristic coolness he choose the constitutional route rather than the revolutionary one.[11] The controversial bill was passed on 2 March 1881 and it became the Protection of Person and Property Act,[12] resulting in the suspension of *habeas corpus* (a legal writ that requires any person arrested to be brought before a court for formal charge or released within the specified period). Over nine hundred members of the Land League were soon arrested and imprisoned without trial. Contrary to Forster's expectations, the number of agrarian crimes continued to rise in Ireland.

In August 1881, a weekly newspaper, *United Ireland*, was founded by Parnell, under the editorship of William O'Brien (1852-1928), a young Cork journalist. It became the organ of the Land League, and circulation sometimes reached 100,000 copies.[13]

Land Act of 1881

The Bessborough Commission, which had been appointed to examine the working of the 1870 Land Act, reported in January 1881; it found that the Act had not succeeded in its objectives, and recommended that the 'three Fs' should be introduced for all tenant farmers. These findings were supported a month later by the Richmond Commission, which was appointed by the Conservative government led by Benjamin Disraeli in August 1879 to investigate agricultural conditions in Britain and Ireland during the late 1870s. The Liberal government accepted the proposal and included it in the Land Law (Ireland) Act of 1881, which was enacted on 22 August at the height of the land war.[14] This was Gladstone's second land Act and a most important one, as it provided for the 'three Fs': fair rent, fixity of tenure and freedom of sale, provisions to safeguard tenants who paid a fair rent from unjust eviction and to compensate those who vacated holdings for improvements made. The fair rents were to be determined by a new body to be established under the Act. It also introduced a system of dual ownership, a concept that recognised two separate interests in a holding of tenanted land: that of the landlord and that of the tenant.[15]

The Act established the Land Commission, to which tenants could apply to have their rents fixed by judicial arbitration for a period of fifteen years, and it was authorised to appoint sub-commissioners who could sit in all parts of the country to consider applications. This provision ended the free contract in respect of rents and came as a big shock to the landlords. The Land Commission was empowered to give loans of up to seventy-five per cent of the price of holdings to tenants who wished to acquire them, as well as purchasing land for resale to tenants. This had little effect because only a small number could afford the required deposit. The 1881 Land Act had one other major defect: it excluded about 150,000 leaseholders and all tenant farmers who had arrears of rent, a provision which favoured the larger farmers, as most arrears were owed by those with smallholdings. Following a succession of bad harvests, almost two-thirds of tenants in County Mayo had arrears of rent at that time.[16]

The Act threatened to split Parnell's followers into two groups: those who had a lot to gain and supported the legislation and others who gained little and opposed it. Most of the Land League leaders opposed the 1881 Land Act because they wanted occupying ownership of all tenanted land. Parnell, with characteristic skill, managed to keep the support of both groups by getting his MPs to abstain from voting for or against the bill in the House of Commons, while highlighting its shortcomings. When it was passed, Parnell continued to attack the government in respect of its land policies for Ireland, and encouraged tenant farmers to bring specific cases to the Land Commission so as to expose the limitations of the Act. At a national convention of the Land League in September 1881, Parnell recommended that tenant farmers should 'test the act' by bringing specific cases.[17] The attractiveness of the concessions for many tenant farmers, however, created considerable tension in the Land League.

Arrests

Parnell was arrested on 13 October 1881 under the Coercion Act and interned in Kilmainham jail in Dublin with other Land League leaders.[18] The Land League responded by issuing a 'No Rent Manifesto' on 18 October 1881 ordering tenant farmers to pay no rents under any circumstances and not to use the land court.[19] The manifesto was written by William O'Brien and signed by Charles Stewart Parnell, Thomas Brennan, John Dillon, Andrew Kettle and Thomas Sexton, all of whom were in Kilmainham, with the names of Michael Davitt (in Portland prison) and Patrick Egan (in Paris) included although neither of them had been consulted. Michael Davitt did not approve of the manifesto at that time believing that it would only lead to further agrarian violence. A national rent strike was considered and deferred on a number of occasions; Davitt felt that it should have been initiated in February 1881 following his arrest. By October 1881, many tenant farmers were satisfied with the new Land Act and the improvements it brought. The 'No Rent Manifesto' was opposed by bishops, priests, several newspapers, including the *Freeman's Journal*, and by many tenant farmers. It was a complete failure and gave the government a reason to take immediate action against the League and, on 20 October 1881, it was proclaimed 'an unlawful and criminal association'.[20]

Ladies' Land League

During 1880, it had became obvious that the arrest of the Land League leaders was only a matter of time, and Michael Davitt was determined that their work should be continued in their absence. He asked the Land League executive to authorise the formation of a provisional committee of ladies to carry on the work. The executive with the exception of Patrick Egan opposed the proposal vehemently, but Davitt persevered and secured a passive assent for what they dreaded 'would be a most dangerous experiment.'[21] Prior to that, numerous women were involved with the Land League, but not in a leadership role. On 31 January 1881, Anna Parnell (another sister of the Land League president) presided at a meeting in 39 Upper Sackville Street, Dublin, at which the Ladies' Land League was formally established. It was the first political association led by Irish women.[22] Thus, Michael Davitt became the first Irish leader to encourage Irish women to participate and take leadership roles in political affairs.

Anne Deane, (1830-1905) a cousin of John Dillon, from Ballaghaderreen was elected president of the Ladies' Land League with Anna Parnell as general secretary. Anna

Parnell (1852-1911) spoke at the first public meeting of the Ladies' Land League which was held in Claremorris, County Mayo, on 13 February 1881. Beatrice Walshe from Balla, County Mayo, a sister of John W. Walsh and a cousin of Michael Davitt, was on the platform as a member of the provisional committee of the Ladies' Land League. Anna Parnell was reported in the *Connaught Telegraph* of 17 February 1881 as stating that the Ladies' Land League was not going to be a charitable organisation but a 'relief movement.' The Ladies' Land League was provided with an office in the same building as the Land League. From its inception, it had a difficult relationship with the Land League, most of whose members had strong views on the role of women in society and deemed political activity by them inappropriate, views strongly reinforced by Charles Stewart Parnell, who never approved of the Ladies' Land League. As a result, the role of the Ladies' Land League was never clearly defined and its champion, Michael Davitt, was imprisoned only three days after its inauguration. The Ladies' Land League, however, established branches around the country and raised money to support families of those evicted or imprisoned. It became very active following the suppression of the Land League in October 1881, taking over the League's functions and extending its relief activities, including the provision of pre-fabricated huts for evicted families and paying court expenses for tenants fighting against ejectment notices.

The Ladies' Land League built up a very efficient organisation within a few months and became quite radical in its approach. This was illustrated early in 1882 when the imprisoned Land League leaders ordered the ladies to call off the 'no rent campaign' and they refused, as well as taking a more aggressive stand at evictions. When Archbishop McCabe of Dublin denounced the Ladies' Land League, on the grounds that it was not appropriate for women, his intervention was greeted with contempt and was also criticised by Archbishop Croke of Cashel.[23] During the imprisonment of William O'Brien, the Ladies' Land League published and circulated the *United Ireland* newspaper. The Ladies' Land League was suppressed on 16 December 1881, and some members were imprisoned for their activities. Meanwhile, the total evictions in 1881 were 3,221, with 16,256 persons affected.[24]

Kilmainham 'Treaty'

After the imprisonment of the Land League leaders, agrarian crimes soared around the country, and Parnell's prediction that Captain Moonlight (a name given to agrarian secret groups) would take his place turned out to be true.[25] Meanwhile, gradually the government realised that they needed the Land League leaders to restore order in the Irish countryside, and Parnell was very anxious to be released for personal reasons. Discussions took place between William O'Shea, an Irish MP acting as an intermediary for Parnell, and Joseph Chamberlain, a Liberal MP who was close to Gladstone. William O'Shea was not Parnell's choice for this role; he became involved on his own initiative and had a big role in Parnell's life later. An understanding was achieved known as the Kilmainham 'Treaty', which ended the land war; the coercion policy was to be abandoned, the 'No Rent Manifesto' withdrawn, the Land-League leaders (including Davitt) to be released, and promises were made to allow leaseholders use the Land Court, as well as to provide help for tenants with arrears of rent so that they too could have access.[26]

Parnell undertook to regard the 1881 Land Act amended on these terms as the final settlement of the land question, and to use his influence to control violence and end the land agitation, as well as co-operating with the Liberal Party in respect of its Irish policy.

Parnell and the other leaders in Kilmainham were set free on 2 May and Michael Davitt was released from Portland on 6 May 1882.[27] The Kilmainham 'Treaty' caused controversy on both sides of the Irish sea. Michael Davitt only became aware of it on his release and did not approve, believing that far more could have been achieved if the land war had continued. He considered that Parnell had surrendered for a small concession when English rule in Ireland was shaken by the land war and believed that a continuation could have resulted in better terms, and possibly some initiative on Home Rule. By then, Davitt wanted to direct the land agitation to a new solution, that of nationalisation. In deference to Parnell and in the interest of unity, he did not publicly criticise the 'treaty'. However, his respect for Parnell's leadership started to wane.[28] As well, some Land League members left the organisation: John Dillon, for health reasons, while Patrick Egan and Thomas Brennan went to America. In Britain, there was criticism of the government for making concessions to the Land League, and its biggest critic the Chief Secretary, W. E. Forster, resigned in protest. His successor, Lord Frederick Cavendish, arrived in Dublin on 6 May 1882, but he and Thomas Henry Burke, the Under Secretary (the head of civil service in Dublin Castle), were murdered that evening in the Phoenix Park, Dublin, by members of a small secret society known as the Invincibles, a splinter group from the IRB. It was believed that Forster had been the intended target. The Phoenix Park murders shocked the people of Britain and Ireland; Parnell, Davitt, and Dillon quickly and vehemently criticised the murders and those responsible for them. The British government reacted to the murders by introducing coercion, which aroused opposition in Ireland and probably prevented any public criticism of Parnell over the Kilmainham 'Treaty'.[29]

Michael Davitt was removed from the supreme council of the IRB in May 1880 because of his Land League activities and thereafter had little involvement. After the Phoenix Park murders, Davitt unambiguously stated that he was no longer a member of the IRB and became a constitutional supporter of Home Rule despite vehement abuse from some former friends.[30] After the land war, Charles Stewart Parnell withdrew from agrarian agitation and directed the movement towards Home Rule by constitutional means, the big goal of his career. On his release from Kilmainham, Parnell made every effort to bring the Ladies' Land League to an end, because he had no influence or control over its members. The Ladies' Land League was wound up in August 1882 with considerable bitterness, especially between Parnell and his sister, Anna, as a result of which they became estranged for the remainder of their lives. However, Michael Davitt had a great admiration for Anna Parnell and her role in the Ladies' Land League. Only for the Ladies' Land League, the coercion policy could have crushed the land agitation, with moderates taking control of the campaign and settling for an amended Land Act rather than the ultimate objective of tenant-ownership. Once again, the vision of Michael Davitt changed and shaped the course of history. The Ladies' Land League deserves a special place in that history.

Anne Deane, the president of the Ladies' Land League, died in Dublin on 3 July

20. *Michael Davitt in New York
(1882).*

21. *Michael Davitt and W. K. Redmond in
New York, June/July 1882.*

1905 and was buried in Straide Friary, County Mayo. Michael Davitt attended her funeral and in an interview with the *Connaught Telegraph* described her as 'one of my dearest friends', and as 'a lady endowed with all the qualities which combine in showing God's best and noblest gift to man, an ideal woman.'[31] After living as a virtual recluse for the rest of her life in Cornwall, Anna Parnell died in a drowning accident at Ilfracombe in Devon on 20 September 1911.

Arrears of Rent Act 1882

Arising from the Kilmainham 'Treaty', the government enacted the Arrears of Rent (Ireland) Act of 1882, which extended the provisions of the 1881 Land Act to include tenants with arrears. This, of course, was a major concession; tenants with holdings of less than £30 valuation who had substantial arrears of rent accumulated over a number of years were liable for one year's rent, with the government undertaking to pay half of the balance, and the landlord suffering the loss of the remainder. This initiative led to the State paying £800,000 in rent arrears for about 130,000 tenant farmers,[32] which gave them access to the land tribunals to have fair rents fixed. The Arrears of Rent Act was the first major benefit of the land campaign for smallholders in the west of Ireland.

The Irish National League

By now, Parnell was determined that the Land League was not to be revived. After returning from a lecture tour in America during June and July 1882, Davitt proposed the establishment of an organisation to be known as 'The National Land and Industrial Union of Ireland:' a democratic body with educational, political, industrial and social objectives. The chief objectives specified were the abolition of the landlord system, which Davitt hoped would lead to land nationalisation, the establishment of a co-operative land and labour association with capital to acquire unoccupied land on which labourers and evicted tenants could be settled, as well as provisions for better housing and the development of manufacturing industries. The proposal contained a provision for the establishment of a network of Mechanics' Institutes to improve access to education for working people. There were also sections dealing with the objective of self-government, financial assistance for Home Rule Members of Parliament, and local government reform.[33] Parnell did not accept the proposal, much to the annoyance of Davitt, who wrote:

> It was the vital turning-point in Mr. Parnell's career, and he unfortunately turned in the wrong direction. He had hitherto been in everything but name a revolutionary reformer, and had won many triumphs at the head of the most powerful organization any Irish leader had at his back for a century. He now resolved to surrender the Land League, and to enter the new stage of his political fortunes as an opportunist statesman.[34]

Parnell did, however, eventually agree to the establishment of the 'Irish Labour and Industrial Union' in August 1882, a body with limited objectives, chiefly to address the position of agricultural labourers by providing access to land and possible employment opportunities.[35] Following discussions at Avondale, Parnell's home, on 13 September 1882, attended by Davitt, Dillon, Brennan and Parnell, it was decided to establish a new body known as the Irish National League. It was inaugurated on 17 October 1882, with its primary objectives Home Rule and land law reform in that order, together with local government reform as well as economic and social development. It replaced the Land League and became a political organisation under the control of the parliamentary party, with a central council and a local branch network. It had a big role in organising constituencies for elections, setting up conventions for the selection of prospective candidates who shared its objectives, and raising funds for the organisation and maintenance of the parliamentary party in particular. Home Rule MPs were paid from these funds.[36]

End of the Land League

Many branches of the Land League had collapsed long before the organisation was proclaimed an unlawful association in October 1881. It was never revived. After the enactment of the Land Act of 1881, thousands of tenant farmers applied to the land courts for rent reductions and had the new figures fixed judicially. Those who benefited most were farmers with big holdings who had no rent arrears, but for many on smallholdings the only solution was emigration to America. After the passing of the Arrears of Rent Act in August 1882, many farmers with smallholdings, who previously had arrears of rent, were able to apply to the land courts. While many thousands availed of the opportunity to have their rents fixed, numerous farmers with smallholdings and a large number of agricultural labourers did not see any future in the small farm economy and sought their livelihoods in other countries. Market forces accelerated this trend for many years thereafter.

Even though Michael Davitt served on the central council of the Irish National League, he was very unhappy with the end of the Land League and never approved of the new organisation. Relations with Parnell continued to deteriorate, aggravated by his new dream of land nationalisation. In November 1882, Davitt made an inflammatory speech in Navan, which resulted in his fourth and last period of imprisonment (4 February-4 June 1883) in the Richmond Bridewell, Dublin.[37] In the speech, he had advised the tenants to hold their rents for at least six months but, if possible, to place them in a relief fund.

Neither agrarian unrest nor evictions ended in 1882, but they did decline considerably. A 'dynamite campaign', launched in England from 1881 to 1888 by Irish-American extremists, caused considerable anti-Irish feeling in Britain and kept the coercion legislation in operation. Davitt tried unsuccessfully to get Parnell to broaden the scope of the Irish Parliamentary Party's programme to include some reforming measures for Britain so as to develop better relations there, especially with the radical wing of the Liberal Party. These measures included general democratic reform in Britain and Ireland, the provision of old-age pensions, compensation for industrial accidents, abolition of the House of Lords, and a reform of the House of Commons. Parnell and the Home Rule Party did not believe that the Irish people would understand such a development and dismissed the proposals as unrealistic. One of the proposals made by Davitt was to campaign for Indian nationalism so as to broaden support for the Irish cause. He suggested that a parliamentary seat might be found in Ireland for Dadabhai Naorogi, an Indian resident in London, so as to give a voice to Indian nationalism in the House of Commons, but there were too many difficulties to be overcome.[38]

Even though members of the Land League, including Davitt, did not appreciate it at the time, they had won a decisive psychological victory over Irish landlordism. With costs rising and rents fixed, many landlords started to question their future prospects and if it would be better for them to sell their farms provided they received satisfactory prices. This change in thinking led to a series of State-supported land purchase schemes and eventual tenant ownership. Chapter seven traces this development, some of which took place after the death of Michael Davitt in 1906.

5

References and Notes

1. Moody, appendix E, p. 565.
2. *Ibid.*, appendix D, p. 563.
3. *Ibid.*, pp. 418-419.
4. *Ibid.*, p. 418.
5. Davitt, Michael, *The Fall of Feudalism in Ireland*, pp. 274-278.
6. Information provided by Dr Nollaig Ó Muraíle, NUI Galway.
7. Moody, p. 453.
8. *Ibid.*, p. 455.
9. *Ibid.*, p. 464.
10. *Ibid.*, p. 465.
11. Lyons, F.S.L., *Ireland Since the Famine*, p. 171.
12. Moody, p. 455.

13   Lee, Joseph, *The Modernisation of Irish Society*, p. 93.
14   Moody, p. 483.
15.   *Ibid.*, p. 483.
16.   Lee, Joseph, 'The Land War', in De Paor, Liam, *Milestones in Irish History*, p. 113.
17.   Moody, pp. 483-493.
18.   *Ibid.*, p. 494.
19.   *Ibid.*, p. 494-498.
20.   *Ibid.*, p. 497.
21.   *Ibid.*, pp. 457 and 481.
      Davitt, Michael, *The Fall of Feudalism in Ireland*, p. 299.
22.   'The Ladies' Land League,' paper read by Marie O'Neill to the Old Galway Society on 20 January 1982, also *Record*, 1982.
23.   Moody, p. 481-482.
24.   *Ibid.*, appendix D, p. 536.
25.   Lyons, F.S.L., *Charles Stewart Parnell*, p. 168.
26.   Moody, pp. 527-530.
27.   *Ibid.*, p. 530-531.
28.   *Ibid.*, p. 537.
29.   Lyons, F.S.F., *Charles Stewart Parnell*, pp. 207-212.
30.   Moody, pp. 536-537.
31.   *Connaught Telegraph*, 8 July 1905.
32.   Lee, Joseph, *The Modernisation of Irish Society*, p. 88.
33.   King, Carla, *Michael Davitt*, p. 42.
34.   Davitt, Michael, *The Fall of Feudalism in Ireland*, p. 349.
35.   King, Carla, *op.cit.*, p. 43.
36.   Moody, pp. 540-545.
37.   *Ibid.*, p. 547.
38.   *Ibid.*, p. 549.

6

New Interests and Home Rule

From 1882 onwards, Michael Davitt developed many new interests, some of which left deep footprints on the sands of time. He travelled extensively, became a founding patron of the Gaelic Athletic Association, got married, promoted land nationalisation, supported the demand for Home Rule, became a Member of Parliament, wrote six books and numerous articles, pioneered a policy of linking Irish issues with the problems of British workers and aided the rise of the British labour movement. In 1882, Davitt supported the rising crofter agitation in Scotland and, a few years later, he helped to start a land movement in Wales. He championed non-denominational education, which was not a popular stand in Ireland in the early years of the twentieth century, as well as supporting agricultural labourers, industrial workers and the marginalised in society, regardless of class, creed, or ethnic origin. He became an international humanitarian, a

22. *Michael Davitt, fourth from right, with a party of visitors at the foot of the Mount of Olives in Jerusalem on 11 April 1885.*

champion of the oppressed, and a fearless exponent of some minority views. His concerns included national struggles for independence in many countries like Poland, Finland, Hungary, India, South Africa and China. However, he remained first and foremost an Irishman, devoted to promoting the political, economic, social and cultural development of the country in every way possible.

Travel

Michael Davitt became very interested in travelling and used his experiences as learning opportunities, some of which were disseminated through his writings. His great interest in international affairs led to a number of commissions from American and Australian newspapers to travel to various parts of the world and report on recent developments. He visited France, Italy, the Holy Land, Egypt, Switzerland and Germany in 1885, Australia and New Zealand in 1895, Canada in 1886, South Africa in 1900, and Russia three times from 1903 to 1905 (the first to investigate anti-semitic attacks there and as a foreign correspondent on the later visits).[1] During the last two trips, Davitt went to Yasnaya Polyana in Tula province to meet the great Russian novelist Leo Tolstoy (1828-1910). (Tolstoy presented him with a brass clock and two brass candelabras.) Davitt made frequent journeys to America as well as to England, Scotland and Wales. He loved America and had numerous friends there.

GAA Patron

When the Gaelic Athletic Association (GAA) was established in Hayes's Hotel, Thurles, on 1 November 1884, Dr Thomas William Croke, archbishop of Cashel, Charles Stewart Parnell, and Michael Davitt were invited to become patrons, and all three accepted.[2] Parnell and Davitt were the two major leaders of nationalist Ireland and Dr Croke was the archbishop of the province where the GAA was established. It was a brave decision by the GAA at a time when it was customary to seek the patronage of the imperial representative in Ireland, the Lord Lieutenant. Davitt was the only one of the original patrons consulted in advance about the establishment of the organisation by its founder, Michael Cusack.[3] In his letter of acceptance to Michael Cusack, written in the Imperial Hotel, Dublin, on 21 December 1884, Michael Davitt wrote:

> I accept with great pleasure the position of patron which has been assigned to me by the Gaelic Athletic Association, though I am painfully conscious of how little assistance I can render you in your praiseworthy undertaking. Anything, however, it is in my power to do to further the objects of the Association, I will most willingly perform, as I cannot but recognise the urgent necessity which exists for a movement like that which you are organising with such zeal.
>
> I have already explained to you my views of Gaelic sports and hinted at plans by which a nationalist taste for them might be cultivated. I have, therefore, only to express my obligations to yourself and friends for the honour conferred upon me and to repeat the assurance of my entire sympathy with the objects of the Gaelic Athletic Association.[4]

Michael Davitt was initially pessimistic about the GAA's prospects and favoured an association devoted to various cultural activities in addition to athletics and field games.

He and Michael Cusack agreed that a great Gaelic cultural festival should be organised on a quinquennial basis along the lines of the ancient Tailteann Games.[5] It was envisaged that it would take a prize fund of £5000 to run the games. On 6 August 1888, Cusack influenced the Central Council of the GAA to accept a proposal to send a group of fifty players, athletes and officials on a tour of the main Irish centres in the United States to raise the required funds. There was very little money raised in Ireland prior to the tour.[6] On 16 September 1888, 'the American Invasion,' as it came to be called, commenced. The Irish athletes and players were given a warm welcome in New York and several other centres, where athletic meetings took place between Irish and American champions, resulting in some new records.[7] The five-week tour to lay the foundation of the GAA in the United States was a big success, but financially it was a disaster, due to terrible weather and the closing stages of an American presidential election between the Democratic incumbent Grover Cleveland and the Republican aspirant for the White House, Benjamin Harrison.[8] Instead of establishing a fund for the Tailteann games, the tour resulted in a big loss, and it took a loan of £450 by Michael Davitt from funds under his control for the party to be able to purchase tickets for the return journey to Ireland.[9] Some athletes decided to remain on in America and started new careers there. Michael Davitt never pressed the GAA to repay the loan and in 1901, when their finances were in a poor state, it was waived.[10] He accepted that the money was spent for a good national purpose! As a result, he took a keen interest in the development of the GAA and was very supportive of Archbishop Croke during the early years when various groups tried unsuccessfully to gain control of the association.[11] Davitt also wrote a preface for the GAA rule book in 1888, and publicised GAA activities in the *Labour World,* a weekly newspaper he edited in London for eight months during 1890-1891.

Glasgow Celtic

Glasgow Celtic Football Club was established on 6 November 1887 on the initiative of County Sligo-born monk, Brother Walfred (Kearins). It was founded to help poor Irish immigrant communities on the east of Glasgow, to raise their self-esteem, to provide opportunities for them to express their identity, and facilitate their integration into Scottish society. The club became one of the most famous in the world and perhaps the most successful sporting institution of the Irish diaspora. When the club moved from its original venue to Celtic Park, the 'initiating kick' at the opening of the new ground on 19 March 1892 was taken by Michael Davitt.[12] A crowd of 10,000 witnessed the opening ceremony, most of whom came to see 'The Father of the Land League'. Michael Davitt was a patron of the club for a number of years.[13] These honours show the high regard the Irish in Glasgow had for him. (The club presented him with a gold medal as patron in 1888.)

Marriage

In 1880, while on a lecture tour in the United States, Michael Davitt reached Oakland, near San Francisco, California, where he was lavishly entertained at the home of a wealthy Irish-American, Mary Canning.[14] Mary, *née* Morgan, a famine emigrant from County Armagh, had settled at St. Joseph in the State of Michigan, where she married an Irishman named Mc Cann.[15] They had no children. Both decided to go to California by different routes but, for some reason, her husband never arrived there.[16] She later married a wealthy local named James Canning in Oakland.[17] Mary's sister, Ellen, had married a man from County Meath, John Yore, before they both emigrated to the United States and settled at St. Joseph, Michigan.[18] In 1867, Ellen was tragically killed in a accident, when the horse-drawn vehicle in which she was travelling left the road after the horse took fright at a dog. She left her husband and their young daughter, Mary.[19] Dr T. W. Moody recorded Mary's date of birth as 3 November 1861,[20] but according to Cahir Davitt she always told her family that it was 1862.[21] After John Yore married again in 1874, young Mary went to Oakland, where her aunt, Mary Canning, reared her at 954, 16th and Myrtle Street, in effect as an adopted daughter.[22] Mary Yore and Michael Davitt met during his September 1880 visit to Oakland and they became friends. During another visit in 1886, he proposed to her and she accepted. Mary, an accomplished

pianist, had a very happy and comfortable upbringing in Oakland. They were married by Father Thomas McSweeney in Oakland on 30 December 1886.[23] Michael was then forty years of age and Mary twenty-five or twenty-six (depending on the correct year of her birth).

After their honeymoon in the United States, Michael and Mary returned to Ireland in February 1887. On arrival in Queenstown, there was a big crowd there to welcome them, led by the Lord Mayor of Cork. A number of bands played a selection of Irish airs. There was another big crowd in Cork to greet them and at every train stop along the route to Dublin. There, they also received a huge welcome, an indication of the high regard Irish people had for Michael Davitt. A few friends, chief among them James Rourke, presented Mary with a pretty residence at Ballybrack, Dalkey, Co. Dublin, which was called the 'Land League Cottage'.[24] It was the only public award Michael Davitt ever

23. *Mary Jane Yore, shortly before her marriage to Michael Davitt on 30 December 1886.*

accepted, but this one was given to his wife. As mentioned earlier, James Rourke, an old Fenian friend of Michael's, was the co-owner with Patrick Egan (of Land League fame) of the City Bakery in Dublin and a member of the Central Land League Committee.

The marriage was a very happy one, and for the first time since his first imprisonment, Michael had a place he could call 'home'. After his return to Ireland in 1878, he had resided for some time in lodgings in Amiens Street, Dublin. For some years before his marriage, he lived at Martello Lodge, Military Road, Ballybrack, Co. Dublin, with his youngest sister, Sabina, who came to Ireland in 1882. After their marriage, Michael and Mary lived in the 'Land League Cottage', also on Military Road, Ballybrack until 1895, when they moved to London, where they rented a house at 67 Park Road, Battersea. (The house on the site of the 'Land League Cottage' is now known as 'Rose Lawn'.) In 1899, they returned to Dublin and lived at Comber House, Mount Salus, Dalkey, until 1903, when they moved to St. Justin's, Victoria Road, Dalkey.[25] Michael and Mary had five children: Kathleen (1888-'95), who died after a short illness, Michael, Eileen, Cahir and Robert.[26] The happiest days of Michael's life were those spent in Ballybrack with his wife and children.

Land Nationalisation

Michael Davitt was treated well during his imprisonment in Portland from February 1881 to May 1882, and unlike his first prison experiences he was allowed some visitors, but could not receive newspapers or any political communications. The Home Secretary, William Harcourt, with the full support of the Prime Minister, W. E. Gladstone, ensured that he was treated in a humane manner. By then, Davitt was a big political figure and his arrest led to major protests not only in Ireland but also around London, including the House of Commons, with a big protest march from Trafalgar Square to Hyde Park, London, on 13 February 1882. Extracts from his pamphlet on his first prison experiences from 1870–1877 were serialised in February and March 1882 in the *Nation* newspaper. Questions were regularly asked regarding the manner of his arrest, why his original release had not been an amnesty, and with regard to his prison conditions and health.

While in Portland, Michael Davitt read widely and one book that made a big impression on him was *Progress and Poverty* by Henry George (1837-'97), an American-born economist and land reformer.[27] He read this book prior to his imprisonment and had met Henry George in America. After re-reading the book in prison and reflecting on the contents, he was influenced to think of land nationalisation as the solution to the Irish land problem. He became convinced that replacing landlords with occupying tenant farmers was not the ideal solution to the land war, as it would not improve the position of those on smallholdings, or provide anything for agricultural labourers or urban workers. According to one historian, Davitt had considered land nationalisation in 1880 but did not accept it as the ideal outcome under a British government.[28] In June 1882, one month after leaving Portland, he made his first speech proposing nationalisation as the solution to the Irish land question.[29] He accepted the argument that land was a scarce resource, which should be collectively owned by the State for the benefit of all citizens; in other words, the State should own all the land and replace the landlords. It was envisaged that nationalisation would give tenants full security in their holdings in return for the payment of a tax equal to the annual value of the bare land and thus put an end to speculation in land values. As a result, the fruit of tenants' labour would accrue to themselves, and public ownership of the land would benefit everyone.

Davitt saw land nationalisation as the best way to address the conflicting aspirations of the different social classes that supported the Land League. His dream was to revive the land agitation in support of nationalisation, linking the causes of agricultural labourers and urban workers in Ireland with those in Britain, and he promoted this strategy vigorously in several public speeches in Britain and Ireland. Charles Stewart Parnell strongly criticised land nationalisation, believing it to be a crazy idea, and Davitt's new objective came as a big shock to tenant farmers, who had their aspirations for occupying-ownership within sight.[30] Together with almost all the Land League leaders, as well as most of the Irish Parliamentary Party, tenant farmers rejected the proposal, and it had no support among Irish-Americans. James Daly and Matthew Harris strongly denounced land nationalisation.[31] Davitt had to accept the reality of the situation; there was no popular support for his radical plan, and he therefore did not oppose the emergence of State aided land purchase schemes for tenant farmers as the solution, even though land nationalisation remained his first preference from 1882 until the end of his life.

Political Landscape

The political landscape of Great Britain and Ireland changed considerably in the mid-1880s. William E. Gladstone and the Liberal Party were in power from 1880 to 8 June 1885, when the government was defeated and the Prime Minister resigned. The Liberal Party at that time opposed Home Rule for Ireland, while the Conservatives were seen as the traditional upholders of the union and the empire. It was not possible to hold a general election in June 1885 because the 1884 Reform Act led to the re-drawing of constituency boundaries and that work was still underway. It was therefore agreed that a minority caretaker Conservative administration under Lord Salisbury would hold office until a general election was held, but he required the support of Parnell and the Home Rule Party.[32] He sought support by making a number of concessions: allowing the coercion legislation to lapse, the introduction by Edward G. Ashbourne of the first full land purchase bill, and the appointment of a supporter of Home Rule as Lord Lieutenant.[33] Parnell was hoping to hold the balance of power after the general election and negotiated with the Conservatives and the Liberals. Gladstone deemed it improper to make any concession and Parnell advised his supporters in Britain to vote for the Conservatives in the general election, much to the annoyance of Davitt, who regarded them as the party of privilege and wealth.

Home Rule Bill

The November 1885 general election was a major success for Parnell, with Home Rulers winning 85 of the 103 seats in Ireland and one in Liverpool, but his party did not have a perfect balance of power. Parnell could support the Liberals and make Gladstone Prime Minister, but he could not do the same for the Conservatives. On 16 December 1885, in a sensational development, Gladstone's son, Herbert, speaking from the family home in Hawarden Castle in Wales, informed the press that his father was very impressed by the electoral support for Home Rule in Ireland and that he now favoured it as the solution to the 'Irish question.'[34] The announcement alienated Conservative support for Home Rule and Charles Stewart Parnell entered into an alliance with the Liberal Party. Meanwhile, the government responded to renewed agrarian resistance in Ireland with a new coercion measure in January 1886. After the Irish Parliamentary Party changed their support to the Liberals, the Conservative government fell that same month, with Gladstone and the Liberals forming a new administration. Gladstone introduced his first Home Rule Bill in the House of Commons on 8 April 1886. It envisaged a local assembly of two chambers in Ireland responsible for internal affairs, with Westminster retaining control of imperial and foreign affairs as well as the army, currency and major taxation issues. The Home Rule Bill of 1886 split the Liberal Party, with 93 of its MPs voting against it. The Bill was defeated on its second reading on 9 June by thirty votes and the government resigned.[35]

The issue of Home Rule dominated the following general election and the Irish Parliamentary Party campaigned in Britain for the Liberals. Home Rulers again won eighty-five seats and the new Unionist Party eighteen (hitherto unionists were Liberal and Conservative MPs), while in Britain, the Conservatives and Liberal Unionists (Liberals opposed to Home Rule) won a decisive majority. A new Conservative administration was elected with Lord Salisbury as Prime Minister. The Conservatives were to remain in power from 1886 to 1905 except for a brief period from 1892 to 1895. In office, their policy on Ireland was to address grievances in the hope that it would eliminate the demand for Home Rule (termed 'killing Home Rule by kindness') and this became the political climate in which the Irish land question was to be resolved. The main achievements of those successive Conservative administrations for Ireland were a series of land purchase acts which transferred ownership of most tenanted land from landlords to occupying-farmers.

Michael Davitt had great respect for the courage, integrity, sense of justice and desire of William Gladstone to resolve Irish grievances, especially his commitment to Home Rule. After leaving the IRB in 1880, Davitt supported Home Rule, without renouncing his earlier Fenian aspiration of complete Irish independence.[36] He accepted that Home Rule was the most that could be obtained in the contemporary political environment and as a result was a strong supporter of the Irish Parliamentary Party's alliance with the Liberals from 1886 onwards.

The Times-Parnell Commission

The Times of London published a serious of articles between March and December 1887, entitled 'Parnellism and Crime', in which it was alleged that Parnell supported criminal actions in Ireland during and after the land war, including the Phoenix Park murders. Parnell promptly and vehemently denied the allegations.[37] The articles caused a public uproar and Parnell asked that the sources used for the articles should be investigated. A special commission of three High Court judges was appointed on 13 August 1888 to investigate not only the sources of the articles but also charges made against Parnell and his party, as well as others involved in the land war, including Michael Davitt.[38] It became known as '*The Times*-Parnell Commission.' Davitt rose to the challenge, believing the Land League itself to be on trial, and became the chief organiser of the defence case, showing in the process that he had a talent for legal work. He made a comprehensive and spirited submission to the commission over seven days: in effect, an outline history of the Land League, which was later published as a book, *Defence of the Land League*.

In February 1889, a Dublin journalist, Richard Pigott, admitted during a vigorous cross-examination by Parnell's counsel to having forged the letters which were used as the sources for the articles.[39] The revelation vindicated Parnell, even though the commission's report was not published until February 1890. The report, when published, exonerated the Irish leaders of the charges made against them, but found that they had promoted agrarian agitation during the land war, as a result of which some crimes were committed.[40] After the dramatic court-room scenes of 1889, Charles Stewart Parnell's stature rose enormously; he was then at the pinnacle of his career and hailed as 'the uncrowned King of Ireland'. Despite their previous difficulties, Michael Davitt fully supported Parnell in his work for Home Rule, especially after the publication of the charges against him in *The Times*, even though he had started to question the personality cult which had developed around him.[41]

Parnell and Katharine O'Shea

Public opinion changed dramatically, however, after details of Parnell's relationship with Katharine O'Shea, wife of a former member of the Home Rule Party, William Henry O'Shea, became known in December 1889. From 1881, both began to live together for short periods, and in 1882 Katharine gave birth to a child, who did not survive, with two other children born to them in 1883 and 1884. In 1886, Parnell and Katharine moved to Eltham in Surrey and lived together. William O'Shea was elected an MP for Galway in March 1886, after being imposed on the constituency by Parnell despite the vigorous opposition of many members of his party, but he walked out of the House of Commons four months later rather than vote for the second reading of the Home Rule bill and resigned his seat.[42] In December 1889, O'Shea filed suit for a divorce from his wife, citing Parnell as a co-respondent and the affair became public.[43] The case came to trial on 17 November 1890, but Parnell or Katharine did not contest it as they wished the divorce suit to succeed so that they could marry.

When the story first broke, Parnell told Davitt that it was untrue and that 'he would emerge from the whole trouble without a stain on his name or reputation.'[44] He was probably referring to the fact that Captain O'Shea was fully aware of the relationship and that the real motive was the expected legacy Katharine was to receive from a wealthy aunt; accordingly, he expected that the suit would be withdrawn.[45] Davitt defended Parnell's reputation in the *Labour World,* a newspaper he edited at that time. When the truth emerged, Davitt and his colleagues were annoyed at Parnell's deception and demanded his temporary resignation as leader of the Irish Parliamentary Party, as they fully understood the damage that could be done to the alliance with the Liberal Party. On 22 November 1890, Michael Davitt wrote an editorial entitled 'Mr. Parnell's Position' in which he stated:

> Mr. Parnell is called upon to make a sacrifice . . . To efface himself for a brief period from public life, until the time which the law requires to elapse before a divorced woman can marry, enables him to come back . . . We urge him . . . to withdraw for a few months from public life . . . In this, the supreme crisis of his career, every true friend of Home Rule, every right-minded man in three countries, will expect Mr. Parnell to perform this act of self-denial in the best interests of the Irish people and their cause.[46]

It was an unpopular stand by Michael Davitt, and he spoke before the Catholic bishops or Gladstone became involved.

Gladstone, under pressure from his colleagues to break the alliance with his controversial Irish ally, pressed the Irish Parliamentary Party to remove Parnell as leader, as public opinion moved strongly against him in Britain and Ireland. Over six days of meetings from 1 to 6 December 1890, in committee room fifteen of the House of Commons, the Irish Parliamentary Party discussed the leadership of Parnell.[47] After a bitter debate, forty-five MPs, led by Justin McCarthy, walked out, leaving Parnell with twenty-seven supporters (the other members were absent).[48] If those absent were present, it is believed that the breakdown would have been 54 against and 32 for Parnell.[49] The Irish Parliamentary Party was split, and Michael Davitt took a strong anti-Parnell stand. Parnell was bitterly criticised in Ireland, especially by the clergy, and most organisations split on the issue, with recriminations lasting for years. Parnell insisted on fighting on and lost three successive by-elections in Ireland: North Kilkenny, North Sligo and Carlow.[50] Davitt campaigned against the Parnellite candidates in each of those elections and both he and Parnell were physically assaulted during the Kilkenny by-election in December 1890.

When the conditional decree of divorce became absolute after the required period of six months, Captain O'Shea got his divorce, while Charles Stewart Parnell and Katharine were married in Steyning, near Brighton, on 25 June 1891. Not in good health for years, Parnell now became exhausted with work and the intense stress of all the hostility towards him. He made his last public speech in a downpour at Creggs in County Galway on 27 September 1891. After returning to England in a very distressed condition, Charles Stewart Parnell died suddenly in Brighton, Sussex, on 6 October 1891 at the age of forty-five. His funeral to Glasnevin cemetery in Dublin on 11 October was one of the largest ever seen in Ireland. His grave was later marked with a big boulder of Wicklow granite, with just one word written on it, Parnell. (Despite her controversial role in Irish history, Katharine never visited Ireland, but she never forgot Parnell. After her death on 5 February 1921, she was buried at Littlehampton in Sussex.)[51]

After the split in the Irish Parliamentary Party, the anti-Parnellite group left the National League on 10 March 1891 and formed the Irish National Federation, with Michael Davitt appointed as one of its secretaries.[52] This group supported the Liberals in Westminster and won 71 seats in the 1892 election, when only nine Parnellites were returned.

Member of Parliament

Michael Davitt resisted a number of requests to stand for parliament in Ireland and England, believing that he could pursue his objectives more effectively outside, but the requests continued. After being elected a Member of Parliament for Meath in 1882, Davitt was disqualified because he was then a prisoner in Portland, after his ticket-of-leave had been revoked.[53] In 1891, he stood unsuccessfully as an anti-Parnellite candidate for Waterford city against John Redmond,[54] in what was a bitter campaign, during which both himself and Parnell were assaulted. In July 1892, he was elected an MP for North Meath, but was unseated on petition when complaints of clerical interference and intimidation in the election were upheld.[55] The election had involved a strong clerical campaign against Parnell, led by Dr Thomas Nulty, bishop of Meath, an early and strong supporter of the Land League who issued a most inappropriate pastoral letter during the 1892 general election. Even though Michael Davitt was exculpated from any blame, the election result was annulled, and he became the innocent victim of the successful petition at great personal cost. The election campaign proved to be very expensive and he was unable to satisfy all his creditors, which resulted in him being declared bankrupt, losing everything, including his home, another traumatic experience for him.[56]

In 1893, Michael Davitt was elected an MP for North-East Cork and finally took his seat in the House of Commons. He was delighted to be there when a Liberal government led by William E. Gladstone introduced the second Home Rule Bill, and welcomed it in his maiden speech on 11 April 1893 as 'a pact of peace between Ireland and the Empire', which earned him considerable admiration in the House of Commons.[57] The bill itself was very controversial and generated strong opposition. However, it was passed by the House of Commons but defeated in the House of Lords, which had an absolute veto at that time. Gladstone retired the following year and his successor accepted that Home Rule was not a popular issue at Westminister. After being declared bankrupt in 1893, Michael Davitt had to resign his seat in the House of Commons.

While in Australia in 1895, Michael Davitt was elected an MP for both South Mayo and East Kerry in the general election that returned the Conservatives to power. He chose to represent his native Mayo, but it was not a pleasant time to be a Member of Parliament, as the Irish nationalist members were split in different camps, with considerable animosity and distrust even within each group. After the resignation of Justin McCarthy on 2 February 1896, John Dillon, with the full support of Michael Davitt, became leader of the anti-Parnellite group. Dillon tried to impose discipline on members and reform the party, but experienced considerable opposition from Timothy Healy. In the House of Commons, Michael Davitt spoke on several topics, including social issues, prison reform, British foreign policy, and in support of local government reform in Ireland during the passage of the Local Government (Ireland) Act of 1898. Despite his many fine qualities, he was not well endowed with those required for an effective politician. He was never happy as a parliamentarian, disliking the club atmosphere of the House of Commons and the rigidity of party discipline. With no time for hypocrisy or ambivalence on a serious policy issue, Davitt shocked public opinion by resigning his seat in the House of Commons on 25 October 1899 in protest against the second Boer War.[58] While it was a courageous and principled decision, it was far from popular in Britain or America.

United Irish League

Michael Davitt became an early supporter inside and outside the House of Commons of the United Irish League, which was established at Westport, County Mayo, on 23 January 1898 by William O'Brien, who had taken up residence in west Mayo in the middle of the 1890s. The new organisation, a response to the depressed state of agriculture in the west, sought the redistribution of large ranches among farmers with smallholdings.[59] It grew rapidly and by October had fifty-three branches, chiefly in County Mayo, and by the end of the century had branches in almost every county.

O'Brien, with the support of his wife Sophie Raffalovich, started a weekly newspaper, the *Irish People*. The United Irish League became very radical, opposing landlords with rent strikes and demands for compulsory land purchase. Davitt remained a strong ally and regularly articulated its objectives in the House of Commons. A frequent visitor to the home of William O'Brien in Westport, he stated on one occasion that he would like to own a cottage in the area, but that never happened. During one of these visits, he climbed Croagh Patrick with William O'Brien.[60]

The rapid growth of the United Irish League sent shock waves to the Irish Members of Parliament and they soon realised that public opinion was moving strongly in favour of an effective unified Irish Parliamentary Party. Greatly troubled by the split and all the acrimony which followed, Michael Davitt made a

24. *Michael Davitt, MP, outside the House of Commons.*

big contribution to discussions between the various groups in an effort to achieve reconciliation, and although no longer in parliament, he became one of the mediators in the process which led to a reunion on 30 January 1900, with John Redmond (1856-1918) as leader. In 1902, Davitt went to the United States on a fund-raising tour for the unified Irish Parliamentary Party, which still had the attainment of Home Rule as its primary objective.

The third Home Rule Bill in 1912, introduced by the Liberal government led by Herbert H Asquith (1852-1928), was passed by the House of Commons but defected in the House of Lords, which then delayed its implementation for two years. Despite the opposition of Ulster Unionists, the Home Rule Bill became law on 18 September 1914, but its implementation was suspended for the duration of the First World War (1914-1918). The 1916 Rising and subsequent events changed the political aspiration in southern Ireland to a republic, thus further alienating the Ulster Unionists. Michael Davitt lived to see the Home Rule legislation enacted and suspended.

6

References and Notes

1.   King, Carla, *Michael Davitt*, pp. 4 -7.
2.   De Búrca, Marcus, *The GAA A History of the Gaelic Athletic Association*, p. 27.
3.   *Ibid.*, p. 29.
4.   I am grateful to P.J. Mc Namara, Louisburgh and London, for supplying a copy of the letter.
5.   De Búrca, Marcus, *op. cit.,* p.43.
6.   *Ibid.,* pp. 43-44.
7.   *Ibid.,* p. 45.
8.   *Ibid.*
9.   *Ibid.*
10.   *Ibid.,* p. 96.
11.   Tierney, Mark, *Croke of Cashel,* pp. 201-204.
12.   O'Fee, Terence, *Western People,* August 17, 1994.
13.   Information provided by Terence O'Fee.
14.   Moody, p. 407.
15.   *Ibid.* Mary Morgan came from County Armagh.
      Source: Cahir Davitt in 1984.
16.   Moody, p. 407.
17.   *Ibid.*
18.   *Ibid.,* and a personal letter from Cahir Davitt in 1984.
19.   *Ibid.* Also notes prepared by P. M. Davitt in 2001 (Davitt Museum).
20.   *Ibid.*
21.   A personal letter from Cahir Davitt in 1984. According to the inscription on her tombstone, she died on 2 November 1934, aged 71, which is in agreement with Cahir's recollection.
22.   Moody, p. 407.
      Notes prepared by P. M. Davitt (Davitt Museum).
23.   *Ibid.*
24.   A personal letter from Robert Davitt, Michael's son, dated 9 November 1979.
25.   Information provided by Cahir Davitt.
26.   Moody, p. 551.
27.   Moody, p. 504.
28.   Bew, Paul, *Land and the National Question in Ireland 1858-'85,* p. 136.
29.   King, Carla, *Michael Davitt,* p. 41.
30.   Moody, T. W., 'Michael Davitt' in Boyle, J. W., *Leaders and Workers,* pp. 47-55.
31.   *Connaught Telegraph,* 24 June and 1 July, 1882.
32.   Lyons, F.S.L., *Ireland Since the Famine,* p. 181.
33.   *Ibid.*
34.   *Ibid.,* p. 183.
35.   *Ibid.,* p. 187.
36.   Moody, p. 381.
37.   Lyons, *op.cit.,* p. 192.
38.   *Ibid.*
39.   *Ibid.*
40.   *Ibid.*
41.   Moody, p. 546.
42.   Lyons, *op.cit.,* pp. 195-196.
43.   *Ibid., p. 195.*
44.   Davitt, Michael, *The Fall of Feudalism in Ireland*, p. 637.
45.   Bew, Paul, *Charles Stewart Parnell,* p. 111.
46.   *Labour World,* 22 November 1890.
47.   Lyons, *op.cit.,* p. 198.

48. *Ibid.*
49. *Ibid.*
50. *Ibid.,* p. 199.
51. Lyons, F.S.L., *Charles Stewart Parnell*, p. 605.
52. King, Carla, *Michael Davitt*, p. 57.
53. *Ibid.*, p. 58.
54. *Ibid.*
55. *Ibid.*
56. Sheehy–Skeffington F., *Michael Davitt: Revolutionary, Agitator and Labour Leader, p. 155.*
57. King, Carla, *op.cit.*, p. 60.
58. King, Carla, *op.cit.,* p. 66.
59. Lyons, F.S.L., *Ireland Since The Famine,* pp. 216–217.
60. O'Brien, Mrs. William, *My Irish Friends,* p. 33.

7

Tenant Ownership

The rents fixed by the land courts, established under the 1881 Land Act, were on average twenty-one per cent less than the previous figures, and tenants who paid the fixed figures could not now be evicted. In 1885, with another crisis in agricultural incomes, amending legislation led to further reductions in rents, after which landlords gradually started to realise that they no longer had secure and predictable incomes from Irish tenant farmers. In the course of the nineteenth century, the growth of a professional civil service, the formation of a police force, after 1867 named the Royal Irish Constabulary, and the establishment of various boards were to deprive landlords of roles they once held. Gradually, they became less important in the maintenance of the union. After the Great Famine, some members of successive governments saw the landlord system as an embarrassment, and a number of civil servants, like the influential Charles Edward Trevelyan (1807-1886), also blamed the landlords for Irish problems. Sometimes, they were just excusing their own failures by laying responsibility elsewhere, and this was particularly true of Trevelyan, who, as assistant secretary to the Treasury from 1840 to 1859, had responsibility for relief during the Great Famine. As the landlords became less essential to British rule in Ireland, they found that they had fewer friends in high places, and felt under siege from their tenants, from the government, and especially from the concept of dual ownership that was introduced in the Land Act of 1881.

Landlords were not happy with the rents fixed by the land courts and slowly began to accept that they would be better off to sell the land to the tenants provided the price was right, while the tenant farmers were interested in becoming owners of the land they occupied provided they could secure the necessary funds and were able to meet the required repayments. It took some time to get both parties to appreciate the desirability of this outcome and to make it attractive for both sellers and buyers. Successive Conservative governments from June 1885 facilitated this process by a series of land Acts, which provided the finance to enable the tenants to buy out their landlords and repay the loans with interest over a specific number of years.

Ashbourne Land Act 1885

The Purchase of Land (Ireland) Act 1885, known as the Ashbourne Act, became a major step along the road to tenant ownership. Under the Act, the State was authorised to advance a loan to cover the full purchase price of a holding, at an interest rate of four per cent, which was to be repaid in annuities over forty-nine years.[1] A sum of five million pounds was provided for land purchase and this was later increased in amending legislation in 1888, enabling over 25,000 tenants to purchase their farms.[2] The Land Act of 1887, introduced by Arthur J. Balfour, brought leaseholders within the scope of the 1881 Act and reduced the period for which rents were fixed from fifteen years to three.[3]

The Plan of Campaign

Following a bad harvest, falling agricultural prices, and a general economic decline in 1885-1886, there was a further threat of famine and evictions. Tenants were unable to pay their rents, even those fixed by the land courts, and reductions were sought. After a Tenants' Relief Bill proposed by Parnell was defeated in the House of Commons, John Dillon, Timothy Harrington and William O'Brien, all members of the National League, published the Plan of Campaign on 23 October 1886 in *United Ireland*.[4] Under its provisions, tenants were to seek reductions on estates where the rents were deemed to be excessive and, if refused, they were to agree among themselves what could be afforded and decide on a reasonable rent. The Griffith Valuation of the 1850s was accepted by tenants as representing a fair basis for agreeing rents, but not by the landlords because they deemed it to be unrealistic at that time. Tenants were to go to the landlords and offer the agreed rents in bulk and, if refused, nothing was to be paid; instead, the money was to be lodged in a campaign fund to support evicted tenants and their families. Any breaches in the Plan of Campaign were to be dealt with by boycotting, and it became a nationalist and exclusively Catholic protest, thus further alienating tenants from the mainly Protestant landlord class.[5] The Plan of Campaign was proclaimed an 'unlawful and criminal conspiracy' in December 1886. Michael Davitt was in the United States when the campaign started and, on his return early in 1887, did not become involved, on the advice of Parnell, who did not wish to annoy Gladstone or breach the terms of the Kilmainham 'Treaty.'[6] Parnell still believed that Gladstone was the one person who could deliver Home Rule for Ireland, which was then his primary political objective.

The Plan of Campaign was first implemented in Woodford, County Galway, on the estate of the Earl of Clanricarde, to be followed on a large number of estates, chiefly in Munster and Connacht, often resulting in bitter resistance and in some cases violence.[7] Three people were shot dead by police and many wounded in Mitchelstown, County Cork, on 9 September 1887.[8] Michael Davitt supported the campaign in spirit and helped raise funds to support families evicted; he spoke in an angry and extreme manner at Bodyke, County Clare, in June 1887 at a protest about evictions there which had infuriated him.[9] On 20 April 1888, Pope Leo XIII issued a papal rescript criticising the Plan of Campaign and boycotting, as well as advising the Irish clergy to refrain from any involvement. Davitt, a big critic of the rescript, was one of many to denounce the intervention of Rome.[10]

Disputes on a number of estates were resolved by peaceful settlements, but some landlords, with the support of Arthur Balfour, Chief Secretary for Ireland, resisted the Plan of Campaign, resulting in the eviction of a large number of people; this put

25. *Michael Davitt and John Dillon (behind the barrel) at an eviction scene in 1887 at Coolgreany, County Wexford, during the Plan of Campaign.*

considerable pressure on the resources of the National League. A Tenants' Defence Association was formed in 1889 to raise funds for the campaign, with the approval of Charles Stewart Parnell and the support of Michael Davitt, who served as a member of its executive council.[11] Under the Crimes Act of 1887, a number of the key members of the Plan of Campaign were imprisoned, and the agitation declined over the following years.[12] The Plan of Campaign forced more people to consider tenant purchase as the only realistic solution to the Irish land problem, including members of the government. It was not surprising to see better terms offered in later years to facilitate the process.

Balfour Land Act 1891

Arthur Balfour, who was associated with coercion during the Plan of Campaign, was responsible for the next land purchase Act in 1891. The Purchase of Land (Ireland) Act 1891, known as the Balfour Act, provided an additional thirty-three million pounds for land purchase and a controversial provision that the landlords were to be paid in land bonds rather than cash.[13] The Act also provided for the establishment of the Congested Districts Board to relieve poverty and congestion along the western seaboard by promoting agriculture, industry, fishing and developing the infrastructure. The new Board was also authorised to amalgamate uneconomic holdings by land purchase.[14] There was a new Land Act in 1896, with still further money for land purchase.[15]

Wyndham Land Act 1903

On 2 September 1902, a son of a Galway landlord family and nephew of Lady Augusta Gregory (1852-1932), Captain John Shawe–Taylor, took the initiative and invited certain named representatives of landlords and tenants to a conference to formulate proposals for a final settlement of the outstanding issues between landlords and tenant farmers.[16] The initiative had the full support of George Wyndham, who had become Chief Secretary for Ireland in 1900, and Lady Gregory was proud of the initiative taken by her nephew. The nominated landlord representatives did not agree to participate, but others took their places. The conference, chaired by Lord Dunraven, produced a unanimous report, recommending the introduction of a massive scheme of land purchase by tenant farmers, supported by the State.[17] It also recommended that landlords should receive the market price for their estates as well as some special inducement to sell, and that repayments by means of land annuities should be spread over sixty-eight and a half years, but the precise provisions were left to the government. Almost all the proposals were incorporated into the Irish Land Bill of 1903, which was guided through parliament by George Wyndham.[18]

Davitt, believing that the terms offered to the landlords were far too generous, criticised the bill in eight letters to the *Freeman's Journal,* and urged the Irish Parliamentary Party to table a list of amendments.[19] He was still a supporter of land nationalisation at this time, but despite his efforts, the bill was passed with four amendments and became known as the Wyndham Land Act (officially the Irish Land Act 1903). The Act provided an additional £100 million for land purchase with loans advanced to purchasers by the State, to be repaid by annuities over sixty-eight and a half years at three and a quarter per cent interest.

Landlords were to be paid from eighteen and a half to twenty-four and a half years' purchase of rents for those fixed by the land courts under the 1881 Act, or from twenty-one and a half to twenty-seven and two-thirds for those rents fixed in or after 1896.[20] Landlords were encouraged to sell their entire estates together, and not by individual holdings, if three-quarters of the tenants on any estate agreed to purchase them. A bonus of twelve per cent on sale price was given to landlords who agreed to sell their entire estates, as well as a promise to pay in cash, with a sum of twelve million pounds provided for these special payments.

Despite the objections of some nationalists, including Michael Davitt, the Wyndham Land Act was a significant development in the process of land purchase by tenant farmers, with nearly 300,000 holdings transferred, the largest number under any such scheme.[21] According to the historian F.S.L. Lyons, the Wyndham Act was 'the caping-stone on the whole edifice of constructive unionism,'[22] as the Irish policy of the Conservative governments was called, and the end of the land war. The Wyndham Land had another interesting connection with a Mayo-man. According to Dr Nollaig Ó Muraíle,

> It was perhaps appropriate that the agrarian revolution begun by Mayo-men such as Daly and Davitt, should have been rounded off, as it were, by another Mayo-man, Sir Antony McDonnell, later Baron McDonnell of Swinford, who, as permanent Under Secretary for Ireland, played an important role in preparing the Land Purchase Act of 1903 which within a decade or two had made landlordism a thing of the past.[23]

Birrell Land Act 1909

The Land Act of 1909, called after Augustine Birrell, introduced a small element of compulsory purchase by enabling the Land Commission and the Congested Districts Board to compulsorily acquire land for the relief of congestion. It redefined the Congested

Districts to include all Connacht, Kerry, as well as parts of Clare and Cork. This Act also re-introduced payment by land bonds.

Hogan Land Acts 1923

After the establishment of the Irish Free State, the Hogan Land Act, officially the Land Act of 1923, introduced by the Minister for Agriculture, Patrick Hogan, contained specific provisions relating to tenanted land (that held under a contract of tenancy) and untenanted land (that held and used by the owner).[24] This Act (as amended in 1925) authorised the compulsory purchase of all remaining tenanted land by the Land Commission, to be sold to tenant farmers subject to payment of the agreed annuities. Provision was made for an automatic means of establishing the price payable to landlords, rents were reduced, and arrears due as far as 1920 were written off. The Act also abolished the concept of dual ownership of tenanted land. The Land Act of 1927 funded arrears that had accumulated and added them to the annuities.

The Land Law (Commission) Act of 1923 abolished the Congested Districts Board and re-constituted the Irish Land Commission. With certain exceptions, the Irish Land Commission was authorised to compulsorily purchase untenanted land situated in a congested district, or elsewhere if necessary, and redistribute it to relieve congestion.[25] This was another radical change in Irish land policy, with the objective of endeavouring to create economic farms. The Land Acts of 1923 were very important, with the cost of land-purchase for 114,000 tenant farmers estimated at £30 million.[26] The Irish Land Commission became involved in major social engineering by compulsorily acquiring land from landlords, large farmers, and graziers and allocating it to small-holders and evicted tenants, as well as the landless.

By the time it published its last reports in 1987, the Irish Land Commission had acquired and re-distributed a total of 2.34 million acres under the land legislation from and prior to 1923 for which it became responsible.[27] At least 134,000 families benefited from enlargement.[28] In addition, the Irish Land Commission transferred over 14,500 farmers and their families from congested parts of the west to over 382,000 acres acquired in the east and midlands.[29]

Major Social Transformation

The series of land Acts from 1870 to 1923 replaced the Irish landlord/tenant system, which had operated from the plantations of the sixteenth and seventeenth centuries, with a multiplicity of owner–occupiers. It is estimated that about 414,000 tenant farmers became owner-occupiers of their holdings, involving approximately 14 million acres.[30] It was a major social transformation, accomplished by legal and political means.

Final Settlement

Repayments of the loans advanced by the British Government for the purchase of tenanted farms were known as 'land annuities'. After the establishment of the Irish Free State in 1922, repayments were collected by the Department of Finance and then sent to London. During the late 1920s, these repayments became an emotive issue, influenced chiefly by County Donegal-born socialist, republican and writer Peadar

O'Donnell (1893-1986),[31] with support from Colonel Maurice Moore, grandson of George Henry Moore of Moore Hall, and it became a major issue in the 1932 general election. Subsequent to the Fianna Fáil Party coming to power with Labour Party support after the election, the government withheld the annuity payments to Britain and refused an offer of mediation. The British government responded by levying duties on Irish agricultural exports to Britain, leading to arbitrary retaliation on both sides and the start of the 'economic war'.

The Land Act of 1933 was brought in by the Minister for Agriculture, James Ryan (1891-1970), to address the huge arrears in annuity payments that had accumulated. The Act authorised the clearance of all arrears from before 1930 and funded those after that date, with all annuities reduced by fifty per cent because of the 'economic war.' The Land Commission was given further powers to compulsorily acquire land for the landless and for those who needed more. (There were other later land Acts in Ireland dealing mainly with the relief of congestion, the price to be paid for holdings and methods of payment).

The dispute over the land annuities payable to Britain was finally resolved in 1938, as one of the terms of the Anglo-Irish Agreement, when a single payment of ten million pounds was agreed as a final settlement. After a long struggle, the Irish land question was finally settled.

7

References and Notes

1. Lyons, F.S.L., *Ireland Since the Famine*, p. 181.
2. *Ibid.*
3. *Ibid.*, p. 193.
4. *Ibid.*, p. 188.
5. *Ibid.*, p. 188-189.
6. King, Carla, *Michael Davitt*, p. 49.
7. Lyons, *op.cit.*, p. 189.
    See Geary, Lawrence M., *The Plan of Campaign 1886-1891*.
8. *Ibid.*, p. 192.
9. Geary, Lawrence M., *The Plan of Campaign 1886-1891*, p. 74.
10. Lyons, *op.cit.*, p. 190
11. King, Carla, *op.cit.*, p. 50.
12. Lyons, *op.cit.*, p. 189.
13. *Ibid.*, pp. 204-205.
14. *Ibid.*, p. 205.
15. *Ibid.*, p. 212.
16. *Ibid.*, p. 218
17. *Ibid.*
18. *Ibid.*
19. Sheehy–Skeffington, F., *Michael Davitt: Revolutionary, Agitator, and Labour Leader*, p. 179.
20. Lyons, *op.cit.*, p. 219.
21. Lee, Joseph, 'The Land War' in De Paor, Liam, *Milestones in Irish History*, p. 114.
22. Lyons, *op.cit.*, p. 219.
23. 'An Outline History of County Mayo,' in O'Hara, Bernard, (ed.), *Mayo: Aspects of its Heritage*, p. 28.

Note: Antony McDonnell (1844-1925) was born at Shragh, near Charlestown, County Mayo.

24   It was called after Patrick Hogan (1891-1936), Minister for Agriculture in the Irish Free State from 1922 to 1932.

25   Lyons, *op.cit.*, p. 606.
      See also a study of the 1923 Land Acts and subsequent developments in Dooley, Terence, *The Land for the People*.

26   Dooley, Terence, *op.cit.*, p. 19.

27   *Ibid.*, p. 231.(To convert to hectares multiply by 0.4047).

28   *Ibid.*

29   *Ibid.*, p. 20.

30   *Final Report of Inter–Departmental Committee on Land Structure Reform*, p. 19.

31   Peadar O'Donnell, a frequent visitor to Mayo, visited the county for the last time on 23 May 1984 for the opening of the Michael Davitt Museum and Centre at Straide. After his death in 1986, his cremated remains were buried in Kilconduff Cemetery, Swinford, with his wife, a native of the area, who died in 1969.

8

Author

Michael Davitt was a prolific writer with a phenomenal output. In addition to numerous contributions to the *Freeman's Journal*, the *Irishman* and the *Nation*, he wrote articles on commission for various American, Canadian, Australian and English newspapers. These constitute a huge part of his writing and were the main sources of his livelihood until near the end of his life, when his wife received a legacy from her wealthy Californian aunt, Mary Canning.[1] In addition to many minor pamphlets, he wrote six books: *Leaves from a Prison Diary, Defence of the Land League, Life and Progress in Australasia, The Boer Fight for Freedom, Within the Pale: The True Story of Anti-Semitic Persecution in Russia* and *The Fall of Feudalism in Ireland*.[2]

Leaves from a Prison Diary

While *Leaves from a Prison Diary* (1885) was Michael Davitt's first book, it was not his first publication. After his release from Dartmoor in December 1877, he recorded his experiences of prison and by May 1878 had published a pamphlet entitled *The Prison Life of Michael Davitt*.[3] When his ticket of leave was revoked on 3 February 1881, he was sent to Portland prison until May 1882. By 1881, he was a well-known public figure and on the instructions of the Home Secretary, William Harcourt, to the governor of Portland, George Clifton, Michael Davitt was treated as a political prisoner and shown great respect, with many special privileges.[4] He was given a cell in the infirmary, which meant that he was segregated from other prisoners, allowed a special diet, given good medical attention and was permitted to work in the infirmary garden for exercise.[5] While allowed wide access to books, he was not given newspapers or material on current affairs. However, his request for the provision of writing paper and a pen shocked the prison authorities. It took seven months and several efforts before the writing material was provided, a privilege without precedent in English convict prisons, but the prison governor was required to read everything he wrote.[6] On his release from Portland, he recovered all the manuscript pages which had been given to the governor on a regular basis. These were the circumstances in which large sections of *Leaves from a Prison Diary* were written.

Leaves from a Prison Diary consists of a series of essays or lectures to an imaginary solitary blackbird. Shortly after his arrival in Portland, Michael Davitt was given a blackbird, with the permission of the governor, and it became his faithful companion for a few months, but escaped before writing began.[7] The book, with a secondary title, *Lectures to a "Solitary" Audience,* is dedicated:

> To the memory of the little confiding friend whose playful moods and loving familiarity helped to cheer the solitude of a convict cell;
> To my,
> Pet Blackbird "Joe".

The book is divided into three parts: the first, entitled 'Criminal Life and Character', consists of twenty 'lectures', the second, on 'Social Evils and Suggested Remedies' has eleven lectures, and the third, 'Political Crime and Political Justice, three'.[8] Parts one and three, with some changes, came from the material drafted in Portland by Michael Davitt, but it is likely that part two was written after his release.[9] Based on wide reading and deep reflection while in prison, it is his most interesting book, with his thoughts on a wide range of topics, most of them way in advance of any of his contemporaries.

In volume one of the book, Davitt considered his experience of prisons and their inmates. Starting with the official classification of convicts by their behaviour in prison, he discussed the various types in each class according to their crimes. He was appalled by the barbarity and harshness of the system with its punitive emphasis. His chief concern was exploring issues relating to wealth, opportunity, poverty, environment and crime. After questioning what turned people into criminals, his solutions were the elimination of poverty and the development of good educational opportunities for all. In his view, prisons should become institutions to promote rehabilitation, and commence with the provision of suitable reading material in a 'judiciously stocked' library, with carefully selected novels and biographies, which could inspire truth, honesty and the desire to lead good lives, as well as providing the surest guarantees of worldly happiness and prosperity.[10]

Volume two of the book contained Davitt's thinking on a range of topics, including education, land nationalisation and political affairs. A strong believer in the value of education, he was convinced that the failure to develop the talents of young people was the most appalling of all wastes,[11] and that many youths developed delinquent ways because of poor education. He recommended the wide provision of local 'elementary schools', incorporating kindergarten, ordinary elementary education and manual instruction in the rudiments of a trade or an art for four to six year old children. This was to be followed to the age of thirteen with a broad general curriculum, including music, drawing and technical instruction adapted to local needs for boys and girls.[12] After deploring the miserable provision made for the education of girls, he went on to say:

> It is gratifying to observe that the early education of boys is being gradually adapted to what are regarded as likely to be his necessities in after life (*sic*); but when we compare this with what is being done for girls with the same view, we must surely blush for shame.[13]

He predicted: 'In the near future, women will be a far more important factor in both the industrial and political mechanism of society than they are now, and it would be well that this should be the case.'[14] Davitt recommended co-educational higher elementary schools for thirteen to fifteen-year olds, to provide a broad curriculum and technical instruction in the trades and occupations predominant in the locality of the school. According to him, 'these institutions should be perfect in every respect', with good classrooms, common-rooms, workshops, dining-rooms, recreational grounds and dormitories where necessary to accommodate those who could not commute daily, as well as being staffed by highly-trained, well-paid, carefully chosen, male and female teachers.[15] Davitt advocated a free compulsory education system, including the provision of a meal in the middle of the day, for all the children up to the age of fifteen years.[16] The system envisaged was to provide a broad general education, together with the skills required for both girls and boys to earn their livelihoods, as well as endeavouring to provide as far as possible that all young people had equal educational opportunities to the age of fifteen. Davitt supported a generous scholarship system to enable students with the ability and interest to progress to post-primary (then in its infancy) and to higher education (then the preserve of the privileged few), where he saw considerable room for co-operation between the various institutions and recommended that they should be connected organically with the other sectors in the educational system.[17]

Appreciating that many young people would then start their working careers at fifteen, he recommended the comprehensive provision of evening classes so that those people could continue their education.[18] A strong believer in life-long education, Davitt proposed the provision of a public library as well as a museum and art gallery in all towns of 5,000 inhabitants, preferably all located in the middle of a public park.[19] In his view, there should be a public park or recreational area in every town and village, where there should be bands playing at least two evenings and two afternoons in each week.[20] 'Why should there not be a school of music as well as a school of art in connection with every considerable town'?, he asked.[21] He believed that public funds should be provided to enable local communities avail of the services of a variety of lecturers, with topics selected in response to local interest. A crusader for the cultural development of society, he recommended that each local community should organise a comprehensive programme of winter activities, concerts, plays, art exhibitions, lectures, with some financial support from the State.[22]

Henry George, the author of *Progress and Poverty* (first published in 1879) and of *The Irish Land Question* (1881), had a big influence on Michael Davitt's thinking on the Irish land question. Davitt became convinced that private ownership, even by the occupying tenants, would not eliminate the problems inherent in individual proprietorship and would result in no benefits for agricultural labourers or urban workers. He saw benefits for the farmer from land nationalisation:

> Thus national proprietary or State ownership of the land would instantly constitute every farmer the practical owner of his farm, subject only to the yearly payment to the State of the annual value of the land exclusive of his improvements, and relieve him at once of these taxes and rates which he pays in addition to his rent.[23]

In *Leaves from a Prison Diary*, Davitt recommended public ownership of railways, gas and water supplies, as well as industrial co-operation and State regulation of industry. However, he did not adopt a doctrinaire approach to these issues, accepting that some activities were best performed by the State, others by private enterprise, and that it was a matter for each generation to decide what was best, having regard to changing circumstances. The major obstacle Davitt saw to his radical proposals being implemented was the monopoly of wealth and privilege in society, exemplified for him by the hereditary privilege enjoyed by members of the House of Lords and by the fact that only two of the 670 members of the House of Commons represented labour.[24] Davitt believed that the political power base had to be changed before there could be a radical change in society. In his view, a beginning could be made by organising working people for electoral purposes and returning a Labour Party fifty or sixty strong to the House of Commons, authorised to act as an independent group on behalf of labour interests.[25] To further this objective, he suggested the establishment of a newspaper devoted chiefly to labour interests to overcome many issues promoted in the existing press such as opposition to the payment of salaries to Members of Parliament (State salaries for MPs were introduced for the first time by the Liberal government under Herbert Henry Asquith in 1911). In his view, workers in other countries would emulate a successful Labour Party in Britain.

In an effort to explain how Irish people felt about being ruled from London, Davitt, in volume three of the book, asked what it would be like for English people to be ruled from Dublin by Irish people through a 'London Castle' ring. After explaining that any solution to the Anglo-Irish problem had to have regard for the two strong strands in Irish nationalism, separatists and Home Rulers, he outlined his own views for a settlement, which were local government reform and a national assembly. He recommended the establishment of a system of county government in Ireland by elective boards to replace the unrepresentative grand jury system.[26] These boards were to control the police within each county, appoint magistrates, maintain law and order as well as initiating schemes such as arterial drainage, tramways, railways, canals, docks, harbours and similar enterprises. After warning that a scheme of local government reform alone would not stifle Irish demand for independence, he supported the inauguration of a one chamber national assembly in Dublin, with elected representatives from all constituencies in the country authorised to legislate for domestic affairs.[27] An Irish administration would be responsible to the National Assembly and modelled on that of Canada. Davitt believed that such a settlement would receive the support of all shades of Irish nationalism and resolve the Anglo-Irish question. Like so many Irish nationalists then and since, he did not consider the views of Ulster Unionists. Overall, *Leaves from a Prison Diary* is in the words of Dr T.W. Moody 'a book of enduring value'.[28]

Defence of the Land League

Davitt's next book, *Defence of the Land League*, the text of his speech to *The Times*–Parnell Commission from 24 to 31 October 1889, was published in 1890. It is an outline history of the Land League, written in response to the charges of complicity in crime brought by *The Times* against Charles Stewart Parnell and other leaders of the Land League, including Davitt himself.

Life and Progress in Australasia

Following a seven-month lecture tour of Australia, Tasmania and New Zealand in 1895, undertaken to earn some money after his bankruptcy, Davitt recorded his experiences and observations in a new book, *Life and Progress in Australasia,* published in 1898. In 1850, a British Act of Parliament had authorised the Australasian colonies to draft their own constitutions for virtual self-government. By the time of Davitt's visit, there were seven separate self-governing colonies. Deploring the fact that Western Australia, with a population of 45,000, had self-government since 1890, he was perplexed that Ireland, with a population of some five million, had been refused in 1886.[29] He outlined the political system and parliament in each colony.

Some decades after the gold rushes and exploration of the 1850s and 1860s, Michael Davitt toured the goldfields and met some of the miners. He was critical of the money made by some mine-owners in contrast with the wages paid to the miners as well as the poor safety procedures in operation. As to be expected, he was also critical of the treatment of the Australian Aborigines by the white settlers.[30] Davitt explored the land-tenure

26. *Michael Davitt and John Flood in Queensland, Australia, in 1895.*

system and experiments in communal farming underway in South Australia, but he did not approve of individuals owning large tracts of land, which were used for grazing rather than tillage. With regard to political developments, he was very impressed by

27. *Michael Davitt with his reception committee at Fremantle, Western Australia, in 1895.*

the development of Labour parties in various colonies and their influence on legislation. Of course, he visited a number of prisons and was particularly impressed by St Helena in Moreton Bay, Queensland, nominating it as his choice of place to serve a fifth imprisonment if it arose.[31]

The Boer Fight for Freedom

Davitt's next book, *The Boer Fight For Freedom*, is an account of the second Anglo-Boer War (1899-1902), based chiefly on information from Boer sources and his own opinions arising from a visit to the Transvaal and the Orange Free State from March to May 1900. He brought the story up to March 1902, based on press reports.[32]

The Anglo-Boer War between Great Britain and the two South African Boer republics, Transvaal and the Orange Free State, aroused considerable opposition from all sections of Irish nationalism, including Michael Davitt. Prior to the start of the war on 11 October 1899, Davitt addressed a big anti-war meeting in Dublin, with Maud Gonne, Arthur Griffith, W. B. Yeats and others.[33] A member of a Transvaal Committee, which was established to promote opposition to the war, he criticised the declaration of war in a trenchant speech in the House of Commons on 17 October.[35] On 26 October 1899, Davitt caused a sensation by resigning his seat in the House of Commons in protest against the Boer War, which he regarded as 'the greatest infamy of the nineteenth century',[36] and stated that he would not 'purchase liberty for Ireland at the base price of voting against liberty in South Africa.'[37] After receiving a commission from the *New York American Journal* to report on the Boer War, Davitt sailed for South Africa in February 1900. He travelled around the two Boer republics, meeting civil and military leaders and

28. *Michael Davitt at Osspruit Camp, Orange Free State.*

talking with various groups. He was present at the last session of the Boer parliament, the Volksraad, before the British captured Pretoria.[38] After arriving back in Ireland in July 1900, he worked on his book which was published in 1902.[39] Strongly anti-British, it championed the Boer cause and Davitt expressed admiration for their courage in fighting for a small nation against what he regarded as the imperialist aggression of the British Empire.

Within the Pale

Going further afield, *Within the Pale: The True Story of Anti-Semitic Persecutions in Russia* (1903), his next book, was based on reports made by Davitt to an American newspaper in 1903 on anti-Semitic outrages in Russia. A pogrom was initiated on 19 April 1903 against Jews in the town of Kishinev in the Russian province of Bessarabia,[40] resulting in 51 people killed, over 400 injured, and considerable damage to property.[41] (Kishinev, *alias* Chisinău, is now the capital of Moldova.) Randolph Hearst, the owner of the *New York American* and other newspapers, appointed Davitt to investigate the accuracy of the reports, a selection showing the respect in which he was held by the American newspaper world. Davitt reached Kishinev in May 1903 and, after visiting the scene of the pogrom and securing information from various sources, his influential reports to the *New York American* confirmed many of the rumours. He was seen as an impartial observer with his accounts reprinted in European and American publications, which led to large support for the victims and their families.[42] Accepting that the reason for the tortures inflicted on the Russian Jews was the fact that they had no homeland, Davitt became a strong supporter of Zionism (a movement for the re-establishment of a Jewish nation in what is now Israel).

29. *Michael Davitt during a visit to Moscow in 1905.*

Michael Davitt then decided to publish the material as a book. He traced the background of the Jews in Russia and the origin of anti-Semitic feeling there which led to the Kishinev pogrom and many other massacres. After discussing the position of Jews in the Russian Empire, he concluded that the best solution was the establishment of a Jewish State in Palestine. After describing Kishinev and the events that took place there, together with the victims and the attackers, he discussed allegations of government collusion in the atrocities.

The Fall of Feudalism in Ireland

The Fall of Feudalism in Ireland (1904) was Michael Davitt's last and most important book. It is his history of the land campaign from 1879 to 1903 within the framework of Irish history from the time of Oliver Cromwell. While it is very sympathic to the tenant farmers, it shows little or no understanding of the landlord class, except a burning desire for their replacement. *The Fall of Feudalism in Ireland* incorporates some of the same material included in *Defence of the Land League*, and together they provide a wealth of information on the Land League, as well as the motives and aspirations of its founder. *The Fall of Feudalism in Ireland,* consisting of 715 pages, is an invaluable contribution to the history of nineteenth-century Ireland, written by the chief architect of the Land League. It is a fair and balanced record of the period from the viewpoint of tenant farmers, with invaluable insights and some interesting comments on the main characters, especially Charles Stewart Parnell, but with James Daly receiving only one mention. Some of the issues covered are referred to in other sections of this book. T.W. Moody, referring to *The Fall of Feudalism in Ireland,* wrote:

> The book shows a gift for synthesis, percipient generalising, lateral thinking, and orderly construction that lift it far above any comparable work by the author's contemporaries. Its style is uneven, at times pedestrian, but on the whole highly readable, and well adapted in pace, tension, and dramatic emphasis to the changing character of its subject. For a book written in less than a year (1903) it is a miraculous performance.[43]

Jottings in Solitary

While in Portland prison, Davitt wrote drafts on a variety of topics entitled *Jottings.* The surviving manuscripts, consisting of 358 pages, are now in the Manuscripts Department of Trinity College Library, Dublin.[44] One section entitled 'Traits of Criminal Life and Character' became volume one of his first book, *Leaves from a Prison Diary.*[45] Another section consists of autobiographical material covering his family background, eviction, emigration and early years in Haslingden. From this and other records kept, it is probable that he planned to write an autobiography, but his early death prevented this. *Jottings* include sections dealing with such varied subjects as his arrest, the spread of religion, Irish communities in England, Ireland's share of the British Constitution as seen in the government and parliamentary franchise, and how Ireland was robbed of her parliament. There were also sections on British foreign policy, especially in relation to Ireland, random thoughts on the Irish land war, secret societies, an annotated list of Irish MPs of the time, and the education of the Irish citizen.[46] Carla King published *Jottings in Solitary* by Michael Davitt in 2003, an edited collection of material from the previously unpublished manuscripts, together with an introduction and notes. Some material covering poetry, sayings, secret societies and a few other items were omitted.[47]

Once again, this publication shows Davitt's huge interest in education and its potential to break the cycle of poverty and create a more equal society. He acknowledged the progress being made in national schools and in the secondary education system established under the Intermediate Education Act of 1878, but considered that teachers under the national board were underpaid for their important service to society, with their salaries then averaging £40 a year for men and £33 for women.[48] He was concerned at the lack of opportunities for working people to access evening schools in Ireland, in contrast to England and Scotland where the Mechanics' Institutes provided an excellent service. He recommended the establishment of a network of 'People's Institutes', with one located in each barony, to be provided by a combination of voluntary labour and local taxes. Each Institute, with a library, reading rooms and lecture facilities, was to provide a range of evening classes, incorporating instruction in the best practices for agricultural production and household management, including removing all animals from homes, the provision of outhouses for animals, improving living accommodation, by installing windows and chimneys in cabins, as well as the promotion of cleanliness.[49] Michael Davitt's wide reading and intellectual interests are evident in *Jottings in Solitary* as well as his great desire to improve political, educational, economic and social policies for the development of Irish society, especially the disadvantaged and marginalised.

Wonderful Legacy

All of Michael Davitt's books are important, but three have an enduring Irish appeal: *Leaves from a Prison Diary, Defence of the Land League,* and *The Fall of Feudalism in Ireland,* while *Jottings in Solitary* is a welcome addition. They are treasures from one of the great shapers of modern Ireland. Overall, Davitt's books reflect his broad international vision, his concern for humanity, and his deep desire to improve societies everywhere. They are a wonderful legacy to posterity.

8

References and Notes

1. Moody, *Davitt and Irish Revolution 1846-'82*, pp. 549 and 587.
2. King, Carla, (ed.), *Michael Davitt: Collected Writings, 1868-1906*.
   This collection of eight volumes consists of Davitt's six books and numerous pamphlets and articles. Details of these books are listed in the bibliography.
3. London, 1878. See note by T. W. Moody, *op.cit.*, p.586.
4. Moody, T. W., 'Introduction' to reprint of original edition of *Leaves from a Prison Diary*, 1972, p. viii.
5. *Ibid.*
6. King, Carla, (ed.), in Davitt, Michael, *Jottings in Solitary*, p. viii.
7. Moody, *op.cit.*, 'Introduction', p.x.
8. It was originally published in 1885 in two volumes and in one volume later that year.
9. Moody, *op.cit.*, 'Introduction', p.ix.
10. Davitt, Michael, *Leaves from a Prison Diary*, vol.1, p. 183.
11. *Ibid.*, vol. 2, p. 23.
12. *Ibid.*, pp. 21-40.
13. *Ibid.*, p. 29.
14. *Ibid.*
15. *Ibid.*, pp. 30 and 31.
16. The school-leaving age in Ireland was increased to 15 on 1 July 1972 and to 16 in 2000.
17. Davitt, Michael, *op.cit.*, pp. 35-40.
18. *Ibid.*, pp. 35-37.
19. *Ibid.*, p. 46.
20. *Ibid.*, p. 54
21. *Ibid.*, p. 53.
22. *Ibid.*, p. 54.
23. *Ibid.*, p. 83.
24. Lecture xxxi.
25. *Ibid.*, p. 161.
26. *Ibid.*, Part 3, p. 251.
27. *Ibid.*, p. 253.
28. *op.cit.*, 'Introduction', p. x.
29. Davitt, Michael, *Life and Progress in Australasia*, p. 27
30. *Ibid.*, chapter 8.

31.   *Ibid.*, p. 423.
32.   Moody, *Davitt and Irish Revolution 1846-82*, p. 550.
33.   King, Carla, *Michael Davitt,* p. 65.
34.   *Ibid.*
35.   *Ibid.*
36.   Davitt, Michael, *The Boer Fight for Freedom*, p. v.
37.   King, Carla, *op.cit.*, p. 66.
38.   Sheehy-Skeffington, F. *Michael Davitt: Revolutionary Agitator and Labour Leader*, p. 169.
39.   King, Carla, *op.cit.*, p. 67.
40.   *Ibid.*, p. 70.
41.   *Ibid.*, p. 71.
42.   *Ibid.*
43.   Moody., p. 550.
44.   King, Carla, (ed.*), Jottings in Solitary,* by Michael Davitt, pp. xiii and xiv.
45.   *Ibid.*, pp. xxi and xxii.
46.   *Ibid.*, pp. xv to xxx
47.   *Ibid.*, pp. xxix and xxx.
48.   *Ibid.*, pp. 84 and 85.
49.   *Ibid.*, pp. 85-96.

9

Labour Pioneer and Early Death

If Michael Davitt's early memories of the rural poor in Ireland influenced him to organise the Land League, his experience of working conditions in Lancashire left him with a deep concern for industrial workers, influencing him to take an active part in various initiatives to improve working conditions especially in Britain, where he was based for much of the 1880s and 1890s. He was a frequent speaker at labour and trade union meetings around England, Scotland and Wales, promoting social justice for workers. Believing that Irish independence could only be achieved with the help of the British working class, he spent much of his time from 1882 to 1906 persuading working people in Britain and Ireland to understand each other's problems. Even after the Kilmainham 'Treaty,' which he rejected, he sought to link land nationalisation to the cause of agricultural labourers and urban workers in Britain and Ireland. Regularly speaking out against injustices, he advocated safety legislation for factories, workmen's compensation for industrial accidents, as well as the provision of old-age pensions.

Agricultural Labourers

Michael Davitt had a great respect for agricultural labourers and was conscious that they gained little from the Land League. The Land Act of 1881 and the Act of August 1882 contained sections authorising the provision of labourers' cottages and allotments. The Labourers' Dwellings Act of 1883 authorised the payment of grants to local authorities for the building of cottages for landless labourers, with about fifteen thousand provided over the following twenty years. Davitt was very happy to preside at a convention in Cork on 21 January 1890 which established a trade union for agricultural workers known as the Irish Democratic Trade and Labour Federation,[1] and he was elected its president. Charles Stewart Parnell did not approve of Davitt's involvement. The union was not a success, and it was replaced by a new body in 1894, the Irish Land and Labour Association.[2]

Irish Trade Union Congress

Michael Davitt suggested to some Irish trade union leaders in 1890 that a conference should be held to consider the formation of an All-Ireland trade union federation.[3] This conference took place in 1891 and led to the establishment of the Irish Trade Union Congress in 1894, modelled on the British Trade Union Congress which was founded in 1868.[4] While supporting trade unions, Davitt did not approve of British-based unions organising branches in Ireland.[5] The early unions in Ireland during the second half of the nineteenth century were branches of British-based unions, organised on a craft basis. Davitt believed that all trade unions in Ireland should be independent of British union control.

Labour World

In September 1890, Michael Davitt launched and edited a penny weekly newspaper in London, *Labour World*, devoted chiefly to labour interests. While taking an independent political stand, it was Liberal-Labour in tone rather than socialist,[6] and covered a wide range of other material: public affairs in Britain, Ireland and America, special features dealing with politics and social issues, sports, short stories, a letters page, book reviews and what must have been the first for a contemporary newspaper, a women's column.[7] At one stage, it had a circulation of up to 60,000.[8] The initiative showed the interest Davitt had in educating the mass of ordinary working people about contemporary developments. However, because of inadequate financing, difficulties with staff and printers, and the workload involved, Davitt resigned after eight months and the newspaper collapsed.[9] Nevertheless, the *Labour World* gave Davitt a pioneering and respected place in the history of labour journalism.

Mediator

Michael Davitt mediated in a number of labour disputes over the years, in particular a bitter strike of Liverpool dockers in 1889, and a dispute between the Dublin United Builders' Labourers' Trade Union and their employers in 1890.[10] He spoke at a number of meetings of Irish railway workers when they were engaged in a strike against the Great Southern and Western Railway in April 1890 as well as at other disputes in Ireland and England. On May day 1890, he was a guest speaker at the Labour Rally in Hyde Park, London.[11]

Support for Labour Candidates

While Davitt was promoting various labour and trade union causes in Britain and Ireland, politically he supported the Liberal alliance with the Irish Parliamentary Party, but his heart was with the emerging Labour political movement in England and Scotland. The first workingmen elected to parliament (two in 1874) did not form a separate party but were a grouping within the Liberal Party.[12] Later, trade union leaders, especially Keir Hardie (1856-1915), a Scottish miner, questioned the wisdom of a Labour/Liberal alliance.[13] Hardie's work led to the establishment of the Scottish Labour Party in 1888 and the election of three labour candidates in 1892, including himself.[14] Michael Davitt supported Labour candidates who were pledged to the Liberal alliance in the general election of 1892, but after the retirement of Gladstone as leader of the Liberal Party in 1894, he moved closer to the position of Keir Hardie, supporting independent labour candidates. Initially, Hardie had questioned Davitt's commitment to labour candidates and did not approve of his stand against Parnell, while Davitt questioned Hardie's commitment to Home Rule for Ireland.

In his book, *Leaves from a Prison Diary*, Davitt expressed the view that if workers organised themselves for electoral purposes they could return a Labour Party with fifty or sixty members to the House of Commons who could be instructed to act independently of other political parties to advance the interests of labour. To achieve this, he recommended that salaries should be paid to MPs and that a newspaper should be published which was devoted to labour interests. Michael Davitt was thus one of the early pioneers of British labour politics.

The Independent Labour Party was founded in 1893 by Keir Hardie, but it failed to have any candidate elected in the general election of 1895.[15] Following the initiative of the British Trade Union Congress in 1899, a special conference of working-class organisations met in 1900 and formed a Labour Representation Committee for the purpose of electing distinct labour candidates to parliament.[16] In the 1900 general election, only two candidates representing the Labour Representation Committee were elected (including Hardie), in comparison with eight for the Labour/Liberal alliance. Michael Davitt campaigned enthusiastically for Labour Representation Committee candidates in the general elections of 1900 and 1906. In the general election of 1906 (in which the Liberals won an overall majority), twenty-nine representatives of the Labour Representation Committee were elected and twenty-four for the Labour/Liberal alliance. The political landscape had changed,[17] and after the election, these twenty-nine MPs met and changed the name of their group from the Labour Representation Committee to the (British) Labour Party.[18] Michael Davitt was one of the special guests at the Labour Party victory celebrations held in the Queen's Hall, London, on 16 February 1906.[19]

Denominational Education

The 1906 general election brought Michael Davitt into a major public controversy in Ireland and once again he took a courageous and unpopular stand. Influenced by his educational experience in Haslingden, he was a strong supporter of non-denominational education. After the Conservative government introduced the Education Bill in 1902, which was to establish a national system of education with support for denominational schools, the Irish parliamentarians came under pressure from some bishops to support it.[20] Michael Davitt did not agree with this approach and became involved in the last public discourse of his life on the topic of non-denominational education. On 15 January 1906, Dr Edward O'Dwyer, the bishop of Limerick, published a letter in the *Freeman's Journal* asking Irish MPs to support the Education Bill introduced by the Conservative Party.[21] On his return from England, Michael Davitt replied in a long letter published in the *Freeman's Journal* on 22 January, supporting a State-sponsored secular educational system with separate denominational religious instruction.[22] The bishop of Limerick did not publicly reply, but others wrote letters to the editor on the subject, with some containing personal abuse of Davitt.[23] In a subsequent letter, Davitt reiterated his support for a public non-denominational school system in Ireland with separate religious instruction, and expressed the view that the episcopal boycott of Trinity College, Dublin, and of the Queen's colleges were prohibitions which only affected the poor, as the wealthy just ignored them.[24]

On 10 February 1906, the bishop of Limerick, in a letter to the *Freeman's Journal*, criticised the Irish Parliamentary Party for allowing the Liberals to be returned to power.[25]

Davitt replied two days later, and the correspondence continued until Lent.[26] A number of bishops returned to the topic of denominational education in their Lenten pastorals, especially Dr O'Dwyer of Limerick and Dr William Walsh of Dublin, and these were read in churches on Sunday 25 February 1906, with some reported in the newspapers on the following day.[27] Dr O'Dwyer referred to the uninformed assertions of Anglo-Irish socialists, and the pastoral of Dr Walsh contained the following passage:

> A great and growing evil of the day is the facility afforded by the newspaper press, in Ireland as in other countries, to persons lamentably uninformed in such matters to give wide-spread publicity to discreditable attacks upon the teaching and upon the rights of the Church in reference to matters such as education. At times, too, through the publication of such writings, newspapers are made use of to give currency to gross misrepresentations of the views and actions of some of the most eminent and widely venerated ecclesiastics of the Catholic Church. Much harm is done by such publications, for, especially amongst the less intelligent and less educated class of newspaper readers, the mischief done by them cannot be counteracted by even the most effective replies. [28]

True to form, Michael Davitt wrote a reply which was sent to the *Freeman's Journal*, but this letter was not published, after he refused to make certain changes requested by the editor.[29] He then decided to publish a pamphlet on education, but it was never undertaken because of his sudden illness and death.

Early Death

During the first three months of 1906, the last thing on Michael Davitt's mind was the possibility of an early death, but he made what was to be his last public speech at the Town Tenants' Conference in the Dublin Mansion House on 5 March 1906.[30] Towards the end of March, Davitt heard about a 'painless dentist' in Dublin and had a tooth extracted.[31] Pleased with the experience, he returned a few days later and had more teeth removed, including the root of one that had been broken during his first imprisonment and had caused him some inconvenience. Some time later, he developed influenza and septic inflammation of his lower jaw, resulting in a big abscess.[32] At Easter, John Dillon visited Davitt and found him in a bad condition. After arranging for him to see a specialist, an operation was carried out on Davitt's jaw on Easter Tuesday, 17 April, and it appeared to be successful.[33] After a month, a second operation became necessary, and he was removed to the Elphis Nursing Home, Lower Mount Street, Dublin, where an affected portion of his jawbone was removed on 15 May.[34] Two days later the medical team issued the following bulletin:

> Mr. Michael Davitt was attacked some weeks ago by a severe septic inflammation of his lower jaw, which resulted in an extensive abscess and destruction of a limited portion of the bone. An operation was performed for the purpose of evacuating the abscess, and a second one on the 15th inst. in order to remove the affected portion of the bone. This was successfully accomplished and the septic condition has since diminished. Mr. Davitt's rest is disturbed by a troublesome cough, but in other respects he is improved. There is no reason why he should not make a thorough recovery, but, his convalescence must be tedious, and will involve rest for some time.[35]

Subsequently, Michael's condition varied considerably, and regular bulletins were issued by the hospital. He had many visitors during his illness, especially James Rourke. While not in the best of health, Mary Davitt visited the hospital to see her husband, but became very ill and had to be admitted as a patient.[36] As his condition deteriorated, Michael, at his own request, was administered the last rites of the Catholic Church by Father Hatton, CC, Westland Row, Dublin.[37] On Sunday 27 May prayers were offered for his recovery at different masses in the parish of Dalkey, and the following evening, a terse bulletin from the hospital stated, 'Mr. Davitt has lost ground during the day and is in a most critical condition.'[38] There were constant enquiries regarding his condition from archbishops, bishops, priests, Members of Parliament, the Lord Chancellor and numerous relatives and friends, many of whom called and left cards and good wishes for a full recovery. The hospital found it practically impossible to answer all the telephone calls received inquiring about the patient's condition.[39]

On Tuesday 29 May, a hospital bulletin stated: 'Mr. Davitt has been losing ground, but is free from pain, and is resting quietly.' The following day's bulletin was very ominous: 'Mr. Davitt has lost ground since yesterday and continues in a most critical condition.' Michael Davitt became unconscious on the evening of Wednesday 30 May 1906 and died close to midnight, with his eldest son, Michael, as well as John Dillon, James Rourke and a few other friends at his bedside. His wife, who was quite ill in an upper room of the hospital, was unable to be present.[40] The cause of death was septicaemia. His death came as a huge shock to his wife, family, friends and indeed everyone who knew or heard of him. The following day, 31 May 1906, the *Freeman's Journal* published this tribute.

The Death of Mr. Davitt.

There will be pain in the heart of the Irish race to-day at the news we record with deepest sorrow. Michael Davitt's last brave fight is over and done. After two months' battling with death, two months of trial endured with the same high and unflinching courage that marked all his life, the great and devoted Irishman passed peacefully away a few minutes after mid-night *(sic)*. Full as his life was of sacrifice and labour for Ireland, from youth to manhood, and through all his manhood years, rich as was his achievement for her, his death comes untimely to his country, and leaves in her leaders' ranks a place that cannot be filled. His personality, like his career, was unique. His character was a rich possession that honoured the race which gave him birth. It was flawless through and through, pure, unselfish, truthful, and courageous. His passion was a passion for liberty and humanity. When he erred it was through love of freedom. If his judgment was ever swayed by bias, the bias was given by the excess of his devotion to the ideal of liberty and human right that he followed through all his years. He cherished those ideals with jealous cherishing. He was never angry save against their enemies, or against the friends that would allow them to be lowered below his own high standard. In the long and noble roll of men who have given their lives to Ireland, given them unseeking, unasking, unrewarded, there is no nobler name than that of Michael Davitt. Her cause, her freedom, her well-being, her nationality ruled his thought and ruled his life's work. Bone of her bone and flesh of her flesh, all that was his he gave. The people loved him because he was all their own. They had a pride in him, because they saw in his high character, and in the flowering of a genius for humanity that no hard condition could blight, a resurrection of the race that had been trampled into the mire of the West, only to rise again to its vindication.[41]

Will

After his death, there was a great desire among Irish nationalists for a public funeral, but his will contained a request for a very simple ceremony, with specific instructions as to where he was to be buried. Its salient points, which epitomised his magnanimous nature, were as follows:

> Should I die in Ireland, I would like to be buried at Straide, Co. Mayo, without any funeral demonstration. If I die in America, I must be buried in my mother's grave at Manayunk, near Philadelphia, and on no account be brought back to Ireland; if in any other country (outside of Great Britain), to be buried in the nearest cemetery to where I may die, with the simplest possible ceremony. Should I die in Great Britain, I must be buried at Straide, Co. Mayo. My diaries are not to be published without my wife's permission. On no account must anything harsh or censorious, written in said diaries by me about any person dead or alive, who has ever worked for Ireland, be printed, published or used so as to give pain to any friend or relative. To all my friends I leave kind thoughts; to my enemies the fullest forgiveness; and to Ireland the undying prayer for the absolute freedom and independence which it was my life's ambition to try and obtain for her.
>
> (Dated, 1 February 1904)[42]

His will encapsulates many attributes of the man: he was a humble Irish patriot who sought no personal honours or monuments; his ambition was the complete independence of his country; he held no personal animosity or vindictiveness to anyone; he had a deep admiration for any person 'dead or alive' who ever worked for Ireland, a great love for his mother, a love for his own native place, Straide, and no care for where his body was laid, provided it was not in Great Britain.

Funeral

As he had requested, Michael Davitt's remains were taken in a single-horse hearse to the Church of the Carmelite Fathers, St. Teresa's, Clarendon Street, Dublin, at 9.00 p.m. on the evening of 31 May without any public notice. In January 1878, it had been the only Catholic Church in Dublin that did not refuse to accept the remains of his Fenian friend, Charles H. McCarthy, who died suddenly following his release from prison.[43] At that time, the Catholic Church condemned the Fenian movement, whose members it excommunicated, but the Carmelite Friary received McCarthy's remains in a hall that opened off the main church so as to avoid a confrontation with the archbishop of Dublin. As Michael Davitt was involved in the funeral arrangements, he never forgot the kindness and help received from the Carmelite Fathers and could pay them no greater tribute than to request that his own body be brought there.

Despite his own request for a private funeral, thousands filed past Davitt's coffin in Clarendon Street church on the evening of his removal, the following day and on Saturday morning, 2 June.[44] Numerous floral tributes, telegrams and messages of sympathy were received from all over the world. His remains were removed from St. Teresa's Church to Broadstone station on Saturday morning, 2 June 1906, and although the funeral was private by request, a large crowd from all sections of Irish society turned up all along the route to pay their respects.[45] At eleven o'clock, the train with the remains of Michael Davitt started off for the west, carrying the chief mourners, old comrades from Fenian days, other friends, and most members of the Irish Parliamentary Party, led by John Redmond, with one carriage containing wreaths and floral tributes. People gathered all along the route to pay their own silent tributes as the train passed by. There was a big crowd awaiting the arrival of the train in Foxford, County Mayo, where a group of local farmers formed a guard of honour around the hearse as it started off for Straide, with all shops and cabins in the town closed and blinds drawn. Every horse-and-trap for miles around Foxford was there to carry those who came to pay their respects.[46] There was a large crowd, including numerous clergy, in the cemetery adjoining Straide Friary, where Michael Davitt was laid to rest within a half kilometre of the place where he was born just over sixty years before. Fr. Patrick Hunt, PP, Straide, assisted by Fr. Denis O'Hara, PP, Kiltimagh (Davitt's great friend), and Canon Lyons of Castlebar officiated at the graveside.[47]

Daily and provincial newspapers in Ireland, Britain, America and Australia and several other countries carried laudatory obituaries, a reflection of Michael Davitt's international stature. Irish public and voluntary bodies passed resolutions of condolence, all accepting that the country had lost the service of a very special person. Michael Davitt was predeceased by a daughter and two of his sisters, Anne (1896) and Mary (1905). His eldest child, Kathleen, who was born on 7 August 1888, had died after a short illness on 18 April 1895, when he was on his way to Australia. He was stunned with the news and wanted to return immediately, but his wife urged him to continue with the arranged lecture tour.[48] Michael Davitt's other sister, Sabina, died in 1922 and was buried in Arlington National Cemetery near Washington DC.[49]

30. *Michael Davitt's sisters,*
    Mary and Anne.

31. *Sabina Davitt, Michael's youngest*
    sister.

(After Michael's death, Mary Davitt presented a chalice and paten to the Church of the Carmelite Fathers in Clarendon Street.)

A Celtic Cross was erected over Michael Davitt's grave in Straide, with an appropriate inscription to his memory in both English and Irish:

> Blessed are they that hunger and thirst after Justice; for they shall have their fill. Matt.5.
> In loving memory of Michael Davitt, who departed this life on the 30th day of May, 1906, at the age of 60 years, R.I.P.
> This monument is erected by his wife, Mary Davitt.
> Blessed are they that suffer persecution for Justice sake for theirs is the Kingdom of Heaven. Matt. 5.

32. *Michael Davitt's grave in Straide, with the friary in the background.*

Family

When Michael Davitt died, he left four young children, aged sixteen, fourteen, twelve and seven that year. Rearing and educating a young family on her own became a big responsibility for his widow, Mary, but she rose to the challenge: all four were later to distinguish themselves in their chosen careers. Michael Martin (1890–1928) and Robert (1899–1981) became doctors, Eileen (1892–1974) a teacher, and Cahir (1894–1986) a lawyer and judge. Michael Martin, who won a gold medal in his final medical examinations, held appointments at the Mater and Jervis Street Hospitals and Temple Street Children's Hospital, as well as in London and Glamorgan before serving as a physician in the Central Hospital, Galway, from 1922 until his early death. He was president of Galwegians Rugby Football Club and of the Connacht Branch of the Irish Rugby Football Union. A lover of music, he organised the Schubert Centenary Concert. He was said to have died from tetanus but according to James P. Murray in his book on

33. *Michael Davitt's family about 1904, left to right, Eileen, Mary (wife), Robert Emmet,*
Michael Martin and Cahir.

the medical history of Galway the symptoms were more like subarachnoid haemorrhage.[50] Michael's widow later married Patrick J. Hogan, a solicitor from Loughrea who, as Minister for Agriculture from 1922 to 1932, introduced the 1923 Land Acts.

Robert Emmet Davitt was a distinguished medical student in University College, Dublin, where he obtained a first-class honours degree and first place in his class. He was a consultant physician in the Charitable Infirmary, Jervis Street, Dublin, for forty-six years until his retirement in 1972. In the general election of 1932, he was elected as a Cumann na nGaedheal TD for the constituency of Westmeath, but he did not seek re-election. In his college days, he was an outstanding rugby and tennis player and in later life became a keen golfer, serving as president of the Leinster Branch of the Golfing Union of Ireland from 1956 to 1958.

34. *Eileen Davitt (daughter) on her MA*
graduation day. (c. 1914)

After a distinguished record in University College, Dublin, Cahir Davitt was called to the Bar in 1916. After serving as a judge of the Dáil Courts from 1920 to 1922 and as a member of the Judiciary Committee in 1922 that organised the new court system, he was Judge Advocate General of the national army from 1922 to 1926 and then a Circuit Court judge. He served as a judge of the High Court from 1945 to 1951 and was its president from 1951 to 1966.

Eileen Davitt, who also had a proud scholastic record graduating with a BA and an MA, had a successful career as a teacher in the Holy Faith Convent, Haddington Road, Dublin. Mary Davitt died on 2 November 1934, at 21 Pembroke Park, Dublin, aged 71, according to the inscription on her tombstone. She was buried in Plot Y, 11, South Prospect Cemetery, Glasnevin, Dublin.[51] Her eldest daughter, Kathleen (who died aged seven in 1895), her son, Michael (who died aged thirty-eight in 1928), and daughter Eileen (who died aged 82 in 1974) were buried in the same plot. Michael and Mary Davitt's other sons, Robert (who died aged 81 in 1981) and Cahir (who died in 1986) were buried in Dean's Grange Cemetery, County Dublin.[52]

35. *Dr Michael Davitt (son) c. 1927-28.*   36. *Justice Cahir Davitt (1945).*

9

References and Notes

1.   King, Carla, *Michael Davitt*, p. 53.
    Boyd, Andrew, *The Rise of Irish Trade Unions 1729-1970*, p. 61.
2.   King, Carla, *op.cit.*
3.   Boyd., *op.cit.*, p. 62.
4.   King, Carla, *op.cit.*, p. 54.
5.   *Ibid.*
6.   Moody, T.W.,'Michael Davitt and the British Labour Movement 1882-1906', p. 68.
7.   King, Carla, *op.cit.*, p. 55.
8.   *Ibid.*
9.   Moody, p. 548 and article at number 6 above, p. 69.
10. King, Carla, *op.cit.*, p. 54.
11. Boyd, *op.cit.*, p. 62.
12. Moody, T.W., 'Michael Davitt and the British Labour Movement 1882-1906', p. 54.

13. *Ibid.*
14. *Ibid.*, p. 55.
15. *Ibid.*
16. *Ibid.*
17. *Ibid.*
18. *Ibid.*, p. 56.
     (The Irish Labour Party was founded in 1912 as the political party of the Irish Trade Union Congress).
19. *Ibid.*, p. 75.
20. King, Carla, *op.cit.,* p. 76.
21. Sheehy-Skeffington, F., *Michael Davitt: Revolutionary, Agitator and Labour Leader,* p. 199.
22. *Ibid.*
23. *Ibid.*, p. 201.
24. *Ibid.*
25. *Ibid.*, p. 202.
26. *Ibid.*
27. *Ibid.*, p. 204.
28. *Ibid.*
29. *Ibid.*, p. 205.
30. Sheehy-Skeffington, F., *Michael Davitt*, p. 209.
31. *Ibid.*, p. 210.
32. *Ibid.*
33. *Ibid.*
34. *Ibid.*
35. *Freeman's Journal*, May 31, 1906.
36. Sheehy-Skeffington, F., *op.cit.*, p. 211.
37. *Freeman's Journal*, May 31, 1906.
     F. Sheehy-Skeffingon stated that the last rites were administered by Father John McCartan, PP, Aughagallon, (p. 211).
38. All the bulletins were recorded in the *Freeman's Journal*.
39. *Freeman's Journal*, May 31, 1906.
40. Sheehy-Skeffington, F., *op.cit.*, p. 211.
41. Freeman's Journal, May 31, 1906.
     Note: The *Freeman's Journal* recorded his death in the early minutes of 31 May 1906.
42. Sheehy-Skeffington, F., *op.cit.*, p. 212.
43. *Ibid.*, p. 213.
44. *Ibid.*
45. *Connaught Telegraph*, Saturday, June 9, 1906.
46. *Ibid.*
47. *Ibid.*
48. O'Brien, Mrs. William, *My Irish Friends*, p. 33.
49. Sabina Davitt served in a clerical position in the US navy during the First World War, which gave her the right to be buried in Arlington National Cemetery. Formally designated a yeoman (F), she was known as a 'yeomanette'. Source: Gráinne Davitt.
50. Murray, James, P., *Galway: A Medico Social History*, p. 231.
51. Information provided in 1984 by Cahir Davitt.
     The inscription on the Davitt grave in Glasnevin is as follows:
     In loving memory of Michael Davitt who died in Dublin on 30 May 1906, aged 60 years, and who in accordance with his wish was buried near his birthplace in Straide, County Mayo. This monument is erected by his wife, Mary, who died 2 November 1934, aged 71 years.
     Mary Kathleen, eldest child of Michael and Mary Davitt, born 7 August 1888, died 18 April 1895.
     Dr Michael Davitt who died in Galway on 1 December 1928 aged 38.
     Eileen, daughter of Michael and Mary Davitt, died 19 June 1974.
52. Information supplied by Gráinne Davitt.

10

A Great Irish Patriot

From his earliest days, Michael Davitt had a challenging and varied life, with many accomplishments to his credit. However, he is chiefly remembered in history as the founder and organiser-in-chief of the Land League. In this chapter, the Land League is reviewed, and Davitt's role in the organisation, as well as some of his other achievements, his personality, some of his beliefs, and his legacy to Ireland.

The Land League: A Review

The land agitation started as a spontaneous local response in County Mayo by a number of tenant farmers who were unable to pay the rents demanded by some landlords and were therefore threatened with eviction. This response led to the establishment of the Land League and a campaign of organised passive resistance, exploiting the moral power of a just cause and mass solidarity. The Land League rocked the landlord system, resulting in the Liberal government introducing the Land Act of 1881 which legalised the '3Fs' and established a system of dual ownership between landlord and tenant, creating the conditions which led to a long series of land purchase Acts from 1885 onwards by which tenant farmers became owner-occupiers of their holdings. The Land League thus achieved its objectives: protection of impoverished tenant farmers threatened with eviction in the short-term and their conversion into owners in the long-term. The days of the landlord aristocracy in Ireland were over, an astonishing transformation in a generation. Some landlord privileges had been removed over the years, but it was Michael Davitt and the Land League that organised the abolition of the system that had been the backbone of the British conquest in Ireland. For this transformation, a succession of British and, after 1922, Irish governments also deserve a share of the credit.

Samuel Clarke, in his *Social Origins of the Irish Land War,* saw the Land League as a united movement against the landlord system, while Paul Bew, in *Land and the National Question 1858-'82,* deemed it to be a fragile alliance of various classes. Whatever unity existed at the start, weakened as the campaign progressed and this was reflected in the eventual outcome. The chief beneficiaries of the Land League were tenant farmers with medium to large holdings, many of whom only became interested and involved when they saw the potential results of the Land Act of 1881 and the possibility of becoming occupying owners. The ancestors of this class of farmers were able to expand their rented holdings as the cottier, labourer, and small farmer classes declined from the time of the Great Famine. Consequently, they were positioned, following the elimination of the landlords, to become the big winners of the land war. A large number of shopkeepers and publicans in local towns and villages, who became an influential sector in the rural economy, also gained enormously. Some of them were to earn reputations for charging exorbitant rates of interest on credit accounts. Arising from the seasonal and fluctuating nature of farm incomes, many tenant farmers and other social groups dependent on them operated credit accounts with local shopkeepers, because they were unable to pledge any assets for credit facilities from banks. Some of these shopkeepers and publicans started investing in land and acquiring ranches for renting, with angry reaction to this development leading to the foundation of the United Irish League by William O'Brien in 1898. Many farmers with smallholdings believed that the State should have acquired these ranches compulsorily for re-distribution to them, but very little was achieved as the agitation became moderated and controlled by the Irish Parliamentary Party. Ultimately, the land agitation aided the post-famine consolidation of economic and political power in rural Ireland.

Agricultural labourers gained little or nothing from the Land League and many of them went into exile, with their numbers declining rapidly in the decades after the land war. Farmers with smallholdings ended up with farms of the same size, many of which were not economic units. This category were later involved in many political campaigns for land redistribution so as to create viable farms, or securing off-farm employment if possible, or becoming seasonal migratory workers in England and Scotland, a tradition which lasted in County Mayo down to the 1960s. Redistribution became the big political land issue of the twentieth century, but the main problem was low incomes. Ownership of land, rather than its use and income generation, was deemed very important as exemplified by the Bull McCabe in John B. Keane's play, *The Field.* Some farmers with small holdings sold them and emigrated, while for many others a pattern developed of late farm inheritance and delayed marriages, as well as numerous ageing bachelors and spinsters with unfulfilled potential and dreams like the tragic figure of Patrick Maguire in 'The Great Hunger' by Patrick Kavanagh.[1]

The Land League was seen by one historian 'as a rather shaky structure, combining tight political organisation with slovenly clerical administration and loose rhetoric,'[2] by Anna Parnell as 'a great sham' because of its lack of radicalism[3] and by her brother as 'hollow and wanting in solidarity.'[4] Having regard to its hasty inception, the troubled times in which it operated, as well as the heterogeneous interest groups involved, the problems reflected in these comments were inevitable, but they do not give due recognition to the amazing level of organisation and unity of purpose achieved in very difficult circumstances. The Land League never developed a strategy to seek expropriation, or redistribution, or compulsory reallocation of land because there were no ways the various interest groups would agree on such radical measures. All its leaders realised that the Land League was inexorably directed away from the interests of small tenant farmers who had started the campaign to serve the aspirations of the more comfortable farmers who became very influential, especially after the benefits of the Land Act of 1881 became apparent. Matthew Harris saw the collaboration of graziers and farmers as a 'union of the shark and the prey.'[5] It could be argued that this was one reason for Michael Davitt supporting land nationalisation as the ideal solution following his release from Portland prison in May 1882. But regardless of how the various social groups in rural Ireland benefited, almost all Irish people were happy to see the end of the landlord system.

The Fall of Feudalism, as Michael Davitt hailed it in one of his books, was not a panacea for all the economic problems on most Irish farms, as owners soon realised that incomes were influenced by many other factors, like dependence on a cheap food policy in the United Kingdom markets, prices, production, efficiency, weather and the nature of farm activities. Agricultural incomes improved very slowly until Ireland joined the European Economic Community on 1 January 1973, a development that resulted in higher and guaranteed prices for most farm produce. By the end of the century, the Common Agricultural Policy (CAP) of the European Union had produced surpluses in most products, resulting in policy changes focused on a liberal global marketplace, diversification with alternative farm enterprises, environmental management and off-farm employment. Many landowners, especially those near cities and towns, were to appreciate the value of land for development purposes. The number of people employed in farming declined all during the twentieth century, and by the start of the third millennium AD, Ireland's economy had been transformed from its dependence on agriculture to one driven by an industrial policy focused on high-technology, knowledge-based, industry and services.

The Land League brought power into the hands of the people, with over a thousand branches throughout the country, and Irish politics were never to be the same again. The outcome of the Land League brought Irish farmers (except the unionist population, mainly in Ulster) behind the movement for national independence and it became a catalyst in politicising and democratising Irish society. The first results began to be seen following the enactment of the Representation of the People Act of 1884 that extended the franchise to most male heads of households (the right to vote was only given in 1918 to women over thirty and men over twenty-one). The Land League eliminated the prevailing deference to class, inferiority and servility that permeated Irish society, paving the way for the emergence of a modern democracy. Popular support for the Land League and the Irish Parliamentary Party created the conditions which made Home Rule a realistic political objective from the middle of the 1880s By the turn of the twentieth century, the landlords, who had virtually ruled the country in 1879, did not control one county council. Joseph Lee, in *The Modernisation of Irish Society 1848 – 1918,* wrote:

> In composition, tactics, and ideology, the Land League ranked among the most effective and sophisticated movements of rural agitation in nineteenth-century Europe.[6]

In the opinion of Charlestown-born journalist and author John Healy (1930-1991):

> Davitt's great success was in smashing the first, and most powerful, garrison of the landlords; his second great achievement is that, by giving the small holders ownership of the land, he created the foundations of a politically stable society which stood up to the strain of a civil war and gave us the political stability we continue to enjoy to-day. We may complain about tweedledum and tweedledee politics; it is the product of conservative ten-acre capitalists whom Davitt's Land League created. The historian of the left may not exult in it. I do.[7]

'The Father of the Land League'

There would have been some type of a land agitation without Michael Davitt, but it would probably have been largely confined to local isolated disputes with landlords in the west of Ireland. James Daly started the land agitation in County Mayo, with support from John O'Connor Power, MP, John J. Louden and others, as well as Matthew Harris and his supporters in County Galway. The pioneering work of James Daly in ventilating the grievances of tenant farmers and others in the *Connaught Telegraph* created hope that the system could be changed. His major roles as secretary of the Mayo Tenants' Defence Association from 1878, in organising and chairing the important meetings in Irishtown and Westport, in his influential evidence to the Bessborough Commission in 1880, his appointment to the central committee as well as his involvement in the Land League campaign deserve special recognition.[8] It's no wonder that the historian Joseph Lee has referred to him as 'the most undeservedly forgotten man in Irish history'.[9] The pioneering role of Matthew Harris in the tenant-right agitation around Ballinasloe and his support for Michael Davitt deserve to be remembered. He spoke at the Irishtown and Westport meetings and had a big part in the Land League campaign as well as serving on the central committee.[10] The work of John Devoy in securing the support of Clan na Gael for the two big Irish issues of the time, self-government and the land question, was also very significant.

While the pioneering roles of James Daly, Matthew Harris, John Devoy and others must be acknowledged, it was Michael Davitt who recognised the potential of the local agitation in the west of Ireland to change the landlord system. It was his vision, organising genius, and networking skills that transformed this local protest in Mayo into a county movement and later into a national one with the immediate goal of protecting the rights

37. *James Daly's grave in the Old Church Cemetery, Castlebar.*

of tenants and the ultimate radical objective of replacing the landlords with tenant-owners within the law. It was Michael Davitt and John Devoy who pioneered a 'new departure' in Fenian policy to support Home Rule and land law reform, but it was Davitt alone who organised the eventual strategy of Fenian support for the Land League. Without his Fenian background and contacts, this could not have been done. It was his charisma and desire to improve the economic conditions of tenant farmers and other social groups that attracted all the different shades of Irish nationalists into a national movement of moral force to replace the landlord system. There were Fenians aspiring to Irish independence who saw the Land League as a means to that objective,

38. *'The Father of the Land League'.*

constitutionalists seeking electoral support, tenant farmers, large and small, initially looking for protection, and townspeople hoping for a viable local economy. Michael Davitt was the first nationalist to solicit and receive the support of Irish-Americans on a large scale for an Irish cause, and personified the land campaign in their eyes. Many other people made enormous contributions to the Land League: Patrick Egan, Thomas Brennan, John Dillon, Andrew Kettle and of course Charles Stewart Parnell. It was Davitt who had the vision to invite Parnell to lead the movement and the persistence to eventually influence him to accept the invitation, a vital factor in the successful outcome.

The leadership, direction, status, influence and political skills of Charles Stewart Parnell were very important in the Land League. He had the vision and pragmatism to bring about an agreement which led eventually to tenant farmers becoming owners of their holdings, one of the big achievements of his political career, while Davitt wanted to continue the land war until landlordism was abolished. It was the persistence of Michael Davitt and the growing popular support for the land movement that swept Parnell from being a relatively insignificant obstructionist Member of Parliament at Westminster to the leadership of the Land League and the popular support he enjoyed in that role. Both men had big and complementary roles in the Land League. In the words of the late Professor Moody:

> The conception, organisation, and inspiration of the Land League were peculiarly Davitt's work, but in the leadership of the farmers in the land war, the greatest mass movement in modern Irish history, both men were indispensable. The success of the land war is conceivable without Egan, or Brennan, or Kettle, or Dillon, but not without both Davitt and Parnell.[11]

Parnell appreciated the enormous contribution of Michael Davitt to the Land League. In a speech in Montreal, Canada, in March 1880, he referred to Davitt as 'the founder of the Land League' and 'the life and soul of the movement'.[12]   He went on to say:

> Would that I could find words to express to you what I feel towards the man who
> has done so much in raising his country from degradation.[13]

It is appropriate that Michael Davitt, the founder, master organiser, and inspiration of the Land League, is honoured in Irish history with the title, 'The Father of the Land League'. No one deserves that honour more. He also deserves to be remembered as a founding father of Irish democracy.

The Person

Michael Davitt was a man with vision, ideas, a deep sense of patriotism, and a passionate concern for the welfare of all human beings. It was seldom that he was not working for some cause or lending his support to a local issue of concern in Britain and Ireland. His interests and concerns ranged from tenant farmers to agricultural labourers, the working-classes in Britain and Ireland, prison conditions, social conditions generally, the Boers in South Africa and the Jews in Russia. A person with an international perspective, he regarded all humanity as one family, believing in the dignity and human rights of all regardless of race, colour, political persuasion or creed. For the last twenty-four years of his life, he was an international humanitarian, a champion of the marginalised in society, as well as a fearless supporter of some minority causes. His objective was always the development of society for the benefit of all its members, with the exception of the landlord ascendancy class. A man of action, he always tried to change policies and systems that annoyed him, from his first campaign for prison reform to his most formidable crusade against the landlord class. A loner, he was seen by his contemporaries as a nonconformist, but most of them respected his social conscience.

A master organiser, a trojan worker, a tireless writer, Davitt had a passion for truth, honesty and social justice for all people. A person of considerable moral and physical courage, as well as transparent integrity, with a mind too noble to harbour personal grudges, he attacked the social system of his time, but not the people in that system, and throughout his life remained independent of power, honour or purse. Generous, amicable, sensitive, warm-hearted, impulsive, idealistic, honourable, principled, loyal, with no conceit or arrogance, he had a strong personality and was his own person in every respect.[14] Though positive and optimistic at all times, he did occasionally suffer from bouts of melancholy. Throughout his life, he suffered many hard knocks and disappointments, but bore them all with admirable fortitude and resilience.

For some reason, Michael Davitt claimed more than his fair share of credit for the initiation of the land agitation, with people like James Daly, Matthew Harris and others not receiving due credit for their pioneering work; there is no evidence to support his claim that he came out of Dartmoor with the Land League on his brain. It evolved after his first visit to the USA, his tour of County Mayo in February 1879, and discussions with many leading nationalists. It was only after the Irishtown meeting in April 1879 that tenant-ownership was articulated as a possible solution to the Irish land question.

According to T. W. Moody, Davitt also had some defects which impinged on his effectiveness as a politician:

> faults of judgment, lack of confidence in himself, over-sensitivity, impulsiveness, a tendency to extend his energies over too wide a field, and the absence of that mysterious power of command that Parnell so superbly possessed.[15]

However, his faults were few and minor when evaluated against his many virtues.

From Fenian to Democrat

Michael Davitt believed that most Irish problems originated with the conquest of the country, a view which had influenced him to join the Fenians. He grew up in a community that believed in the physical-force tradition of Irish nationalism because its members could see little progress being achieved by political means. While he disliked imperial rule in Ireland, he had a great respect for all British people. His Fenian involvement troubled him throughout his life and left him ambivalent in his views on the use of force. After questioning the intolerance of Fenianism and becoming disillusioned with it, a gradual disengagement from the movement was completed with the Phoenix Park murders of Lord Frederick Cavendish, Chief Secretary for Ireland, and Thomas Burke, the Under-Secretary, on 6 May 1882, the day of his release from Portland Prison. On 11 May 1882, he told an America newspaper in an interview that he was no longer a Fenian.[16] He became one of many Irish nationalists to make the transition from the physical force approach of the Fenians to democratic politics, much to the chagrin of many former friends. Although disliking violence and cruelty, he would not regard himself as a pacifist. Davitt became a democrat who believed in changing society by informed public discourse and he made a huge contribution to discussions in his numerous letters to newspapers. While not accepting that the majority was always right, he believed that minorities should respect majority decisions while endeavouring by informed debate to secure acceptance for their own opinions. Despite some terrible attacks on his character, even by bishops, he was very generous in almost all cases in responding to opponents, by keeping to the issues and avoiding personal abuse. In the interest of harmony and the advancement of causes, he regularly did not follow through on issues or try to be seen to get the better of opponents. The cause and the outcome mattered more to him than any personal pride or ego. After 1882, Michael Davitt favoured State ownership as the ideal solution to the Irish Land question, but this was completely unacceptable to the tenant farmers, to Irish Americans and to Parnell. Davitt, however, was big enough to realise that his proposal had no popular support and accepted the view of the majority, that tenant-ownership was the only acceptable solution.

Home Ruler

Michael Davitt worked for an independent, democratic, egalitarian Ireland, progressive, tolerant, pluralist and outward looking.[17] After 1884, he was prepared to accept Home Rule within the union as the most that could be obtained at that time. His nationalism was non-sectarian and inclusive. A native Irish speaker, he supported the Gaelic League in its efforts to promote the Irish language, but did not agree with a Gaelic-speaking Ireland only, believing that children should learn a number of languages as well as Irish history. Politically, Davitt supported the Irish Parliamentary Party's alliance with the Liberals when W. E. Gladstone was leader and thereafter he moved closer to the emerging labour movement. However, he did not see himself as a socialist. During the 1906 general election he stated:

> I am not a socialist myself; I am content to be an Irish nationalist and land reformer; but there are many articles in the political creed of socialism to which I willingly subscribe.[18]

Supporter of Equality for Women

Michael Davitt was the first Irish public figure to promote the equality of women in society. In his book, *Leaves from a Prison Diary*, he deplored the limited educational opportunities provided for girls and strongly recommended that the system at all levels should provide equal opportunities for both genders. He became the first Irish leader to promote the leadership of women in political life through the Ladies' Land League. Unlike many of his contemporaries, including Parnell, he did not believe that their only place was in the home or their only other work benevolent activities, and in this, as in so many aspects of his life, he was way in advance of his time. He strongly supported equal political rights for women, including the right to vote and stand for election.[19]

Education

Highly intelligent and self-educated to a great extent, Michael Davitt's reading embraced English literature, history, politics, economics, biographies and the Bible.[20] His intellectual curiosity turned every experience into a learning opportunity, especially his numerous journeys abroad. Shortly after his arrival in Philadelphia in July 1878, on his first visit abroad following his release from prison, he explored the historic sites of the city, recording the experience in his diary.[21] He visited Independence Hall, where the American founding fathers signed the Declaration of Independence on 4 July 1776 and where the US Constitution was adopted on 17 September 1787, Congress Hall, where Congress met from 1790 to 1800 when the city was the first capital of the US, as well as Christ Church, where he saw the grave of Benjamin Franklin in the adjacent burial-ground, a man who helped draft the US Declaration of Independence and the Constitution. Amongst other sites and places, he also saw the Liberty Bell, which rang out on 4 July 1776, the Free Library, Fairmount Park and, of course, the local prison. Thereafter, he really enjoyed travelling and loved exploring different places. He loved reading, writing and, when the opportunities arose, attending theatres, concerts and operas. According to Dr T. W. Moody, Davitt had some knowledge of French, Spanish, German, Italian and Latin, which is amazing in view of his limited learning opportunities.[22]

Davitt's biggest intellectual accomplishments were the publication of six books, an enormous achievement having regard to his life and disability (he had to learn to write with his left hand following the amputation of the right one). His six books encapsulate his enormous ability, concentration, dedication and work-rate as well as his desire to disseminate knowledge and ideas for the betterment of society. No other Irish political figure has bequeathed to posterity such a valuable record of contemporary affairs.

Appreciating the role of education as a source of empowerment for individuals, families, society and the economy, he made several recommendations in his writings for widening access to everyone able and willing to avail of it. After his own experience of the Mechanics' Institute in Haslingden, he had a big interest in the provision of suitable evening courses for working people, and supported the establishment of similar Institutes in Ireland in his proposals for a National Land Reform and Industrial Union of Ireland in 1882 to replace the Land League, but Parnell rejected this.[23] Michael Davitt believed strongly in the transformative role of education in developing the talents of people, in enhancing their opportunities to earn their livelihoods, in improving their living conditions as well as enabling them to enjoy social and cultural activities.

Patriotic Public Service

Scrupulous in his use of public funds, Davitt never used such money for his own benefit despite the precarious state of his own finances for most of his life.[24] After his release from prison, he took up no full-time position but earned his living from freelance journalism and public speaking, with some initial help from the IRB. He could have obtained a secure job with a regular income, but chose instead to serve his country and its people at a great personal cost. Being a strong believer in patriotic public service, which in his case was unpaid, his ethical views on public funds are even more commendable. Refusing on several occasions to accept testimonials or any financial support from his friends,[25] he lived a frugal life, with his wife having occasionally to receive help from her aunt, Mary Canning, from whom in 1904 she inherited enough for them to live in some comfort in Dalkey.[26] Despite his financial position, he was a generous contributor to various political and benevolent causes, and especially to anyone in trouble. On a visit to Paris, he called on the Irish-born dramatist, Oscar Wilde (1852-1900), then living in poor circumstances and shunned by his friends following his release from Reading Gaol. Davitt took the famous literary artist to dinner and gave him a pleasant evening.[27] Wilde gave him a copy of his recent publication, *The Ballad of Reading Gaol* (1898), in appreciation of Davitt's work for prison reform.

Michael Davitt was passionate in his desire to change institutions, laws, public policy and society to serve the needs of all the people and not a privileged few. He was influenced by his strong beliefs in liberty, democracy, equality of opportunity and social inclusion. What came to be called vested interests were anathema to him, as he was interested in public policy serving the real needs of all. He believed in fair, honest and ethical public service, with special attention to the needs of the marginalised and most disadvantaged. What he wished for Ireland, he also supported for all humanity.

Alcohol

Michael Davitt rarely touched alcohol, believing the Irish people had a propensity for drink.[28] After seeing the way many abused alcohol at home and in other countries, he was shocked and felt that it was due to some weakness in the Irish race. He really despised the abuse of drink. However, he believed that if the Irish had a fault worse than drink it was moral cowardice. His own moral courage was evident in the range of unpopular minority causes he championed in the public press, from land nationalisation to non-denominational education.

Christian

Michael Davitt, a Christian with a great respect for all denominations, was a practising Catholic for most of his life and received the last rites of the church before his death.[29] This did not stop him from taking public stands on issues that left him at odds with some Irish bishops and clergy, and he had the courage to defy 'the lion of the west', Archbishop John MacHale, about the Westport public meeting on 8 June 1879. The following month, another letter in the name of Archbishop MacHale, which was published in the *Freeman's Journal*, referred to Davitt contemptuously as an 'unknown, strolling man'. Davitt's reply showed that he was deeply hurt having regard to all the sacrifices made by himself and his family and also illustrated his magnanimous nature in responding to an opponent:

> As one who has taken part in the meeting to which His Grace refers, I beg respectfully to say that I am neither an unknown nor a strolling man in the west... Some twenty-five years ago my father was evicted from a small holding near the parish of Straide, in Mayo, because unable to pay a rent which the crippled state of his resources, after struggling through the famine years, rendered impossible. Trials and sufferings in exile for a quarter of a century, in which I became physically disabled for life, a father's grave dug beneath American soil, myself the only member of the family ever destined to live or die in Ireland, this privilege existing only by virtue of "ticket-of-leave", are the consequences which followed that eviction... As for any... advancement on the people's shoulders, the only one I am likely to obtain by their patronage will be in the direction of oakum-picking in Millbank, or stone-breaking in Dartmoor Convict Prison; preferments which, with their indignities and suffering, I am in a fair way of being convinced, are more easily borne than the imputations, insults, and injuries which the participant in Irish politics receives for his endeavours.[30]

In February 1906, Michael Davitt became engaged in a public debate about non-denominational education with the bishop of Limerick and others. With no trace of sectarianism and with respect for people of all religions and none, he was not anti-clerical and had many great friends in the clergy, including at least two prelates, Dr Croke, archbishop of Cashel, and Dr Duggan, bishop of Clonfert. In 1904, a Redemptorist priest in Limerick, Father Creagh, launched a tirade of sermons against the Jewish community of that city, accusing them of charging exorbitant rates of interest on goods and calling for a boycott against them. Davitt was quick to publicly criticise the attacks on the Jews in Limerick in a letter to the *Freeman's Journal*, but the boycott continued for nearly two years, leading to the exodus of many Jews from the city.[31]

Respect and Affection

A loyal son, Michael Davitt fully appreciated the suffering his imprisonment caused his parents, and he was also a caring and supportive brother to his three sisters. A devoted husband and an exemplary father, tender and patient,[32] he was an exceptional man by any standards. Given his background, circumstances, opportunities in life and career path, one can only speak of the man and his achievements in superlative terms. During his lifetime from 1879, no public figure commanded more respect and affection among Irish people at home and abroad than Michael Davitt. He received many public tributes around the world and in his native country, including becoming a freeman of Limerick on 14 April 1884.

However, there are some historians who regard the Land League as a failure because land nationalisation was not achieved, but such a judgment takes an unfair and incorrect view of the objectives and development of the Land League. Land nationalisation was not the original objective of Michael Davitt, or of the National Land League of Mayo, nor of its successor, the National Land League. It was only placed on the national political agenda by Michael Davitt following his release from Portland in May 1882, but was no more acceptable to the tenant farmers of that period than it would be to their successors today. Furthermore, as Professor Thomas P. O'Neill of University College, Galway, said in Irishtown on 22 April 1979:

> The Irish farmers had a sense of ownership in the soil on which the sweat of generations had been spilled. They had no wish to exchange Lord Clanmorris, or Lord Arran or anybody else, for a British State represented by Queen Victoria.[33]

It is true that many tenant farmers and/or their sons and daughters had to emigrate from *post* Land League Ireland, due to market forces and the under-developed state of the economy over which Michael Davitt had no control. He was eclipsed by the men and women of 1916–1921; in that period and for some decades thereafter there was a tendency to define patriotism in such a narrow fashion as to exclude the likes of Davitt and many of his contemporaries.

The building occupied by the Department of Labour in Mespil Road, Dublin, was named 'Davitt House' in 1975; the government building in Castlebar, opened on 28 June 1976 by the then Taoiseach, Liam Cosgrave, TD, was called 'Davitt House', and a room in the Castlebar Campus of the Galway-Mayo Institute of Technology was named after him in 1995. Davitt's GAA Club in Ballindine and Moy Davitt's GAA Club (Bohola, Straide, Foxford) in County Mayo, together with clubs in other counties and a number of GAA pitches, as well as some places around the country were named in his honour. The bridge from Achill Island to the mainland was named after him. In his native Mayo, his framed photograph was displayed in a prominent place in many homes until John Fitzgerald Kennedy and Pope John XXIII replaced him during the 1960s.

Numerous public figures have recorded their respect and affection for Michael Davitt, and some referred to his influence on their careers, including James Connolly (1868-1916), the trade unionist and 1916 leader, David Lloyd-George (1863-1945), British Prime Minister 1916-1922, and Mahatma Gandhi (1869-1948), the Indian national leader.

39. *Grainne Davitt (granddaughter of Michael Davitt) left and Arun Gandhi (grandson of Mahatma Gandhi) together with Nancy Smyth, secretary of The Michael Davitt Memorial Association, looking at exhibits in the Michael Davitt Memorial Museum, Straide, in 1991.*

A Great Irish Patriot

The publication of Theodore William Moody's great book, *Davitt and Irish Revolution 1846–'82* (1981) has focused more scholarly attention on Davitt and elevated him to an exalted place in Irish history. Moody's concluding comments on Davitt's life are instructive:

> But in the estimation of Irishmen and of innumerable others all over the world his faults counted for very little in the scale against his great-heartedness, his self-sacrifice, and his invincible courage. He did not seek power or glory or money but he won gratitude and respect and love in full measure.[34]

For Francis Sheehy-Skeffington, Davitt was 'the greatest Irishman of the nineteenth century'.[35] In a tribute after his death the chairperson of the British Labour Party from 1906 to 1908, Keir Hardie, wrote, 'the people of Ireland owe more to him than to any of the rebel chiefs of their race'.[36] According to a contemporary historian Carla King,

> It is thus in the breadth of his vision as an Irish nationalist, social thinker and internationalist, that Davitt may fairly be seen as a founding father of Irish democracy.[37]

120

John Healy, in a tribute to Michael Davitt in *The Western Journal* in August 1978, wrote:

> He more than any other has shaped modern Ireland and left it what is it to-day: a prospering island on the edge of Europe with the great gift of political stability without which there can not be any progress.[38]

Michael Davitt's legacy to Ireland was immense: a country almost free of the landlord ascendancy class, once 'the political garrison of the union,' occupying-ownership of the land by a multiplicity of Irish farmers, as well as a foundation for the development of an independent, inclusive, democratic State, and a role model for patriotic public service. The abolition of the landlord ascendancy in Ireland, Davitt's primary objective, weakened the union with the United Kingdom, advanced the interests of Irish nationalism, and in the process sowed the seeds for a modern democracy. Thus, Michael Davitt can be seen as a founder of Irish democracy. His legacy should also have engendered a desire for a progressive, caring, outward looking, society, based on a first-class educational system, equality of opportunity and social inclusion. However, his radical views on social policies had little effect in the new State. Michael Davitt was one of the greatest patriots, if not the greatest, to grace the pages of Irish history. Irishmen and Irishwomen, and indeed all humanity, have every reason to revere the memory of this extraordinary son of County Mayo.

10

References and Notes

1. Kavanagh, Patrick, *Collected Poems*.
2. Foster, R.F., *Modern Ireland 1600-1972*, p. 411.
3. *The Tale of a Great Sham*, edited with an Introduction by Dana Hearne.
4. O'Shea, Katharine, *Charles Stewart Parnell: His Love Story and Political Life*, Vol. 1, pp. 235-236.
5. Foster, R. F., *op.cit.*, p. 411.
6. p. 89.
7. *The Irish Times*, October 1979.
8. See Jordan Jr., Donald, E., *Land and Popular Politics in Ireland: County Mayo from the Plantation to the Land War*, pp. 277.
   Note: After becoming disillusioned with the centralisation and later direction of the Land League, James Daly became estranged from it. He and Davitt were never close friends and later drifted further apart. Daly opposed Davitt's land nationalisation proposal. He sold the *Connacht Telegraph* to Thomas Gillespie in 1892 and became a full-time farmer. James Daly died on 22 March 1910, aged 74, and was buried in the Old Church Cemetery in Castlebar. His wife, Honoria, *née* O Donnell from Mulrany (*alias* Mullaranny), died on 25 November 1930, aged 86, and was buried in the same grave as her husband.
9. Lee, Joseph, *The Modernisation of Irish Society 1845-1918*, p. 558.
10. Matthew Harris served as an MP. for East Galway from 1885 until his death in 1890.
   He was buried in Creagh cemetery in Ballinasloe, County Galway. Michael Davitt attended his funeral and later was one of the generous subscribers to the Harris memorial in the cemetery.
11. Moody, T.,W., *Davitt and Irish Revolution 1846-1882*, p. 558.
12. *Ibid.*, p. 357.
13. *Ibid.*, p. 358.

14. *Ibid.*, p. 551.
15. *Ibid.*, p. 558.
16. *Ibid.*, p. 536.
17. *Ibid.*, p. 556.
18. Sheehy-Skeffington, F., *Michael Davitt*, p. 191.
19. Davitt, Michael, *Life and Progress in Australasia*, pp. 336-337.
20. Moody, *op.cit.*, p. 504.
21. *Ibid.*, p. 227.
22. *Ibid.*, p. 504.
23. King, Carla, (ed.,) *Jottings in Solitary* by Michael Davitt, p. 253.
24. Moody, *op.cit.,* p. 552.
25. Charles Stewart Parnell received over £37,000 from a testimonial in December 1883.
     Source: King, Carla, *Michael Davitt*, p. 3.
26. Moody, *op.cit.*, p. 552.
27. O'Brien, Mrs. William, *My Irish Friends*, p. 37.
28. *Moody.*, p. 551.
29. *Ibid.,* p. 553.
30. Quoted in Sheehy-Skeffington, F., *Michael Davitt*, p. 85.
31. For the story of the boycott, see
     Keogh, Dermot, and McCarthy, Andrew, *Limerick Boycott 1904: Anti-Semitism in Ireland.*
32. O'Brien, Mrs. William, *My Irish Friends*, p. 32.
33. Speech delivered at the centenary of land meeting in Irishtown.
34. Moody, T., W., *Davitt and Irish Revolution 1846-'82*, p. 558.
35. *Michael Davitt: Revolutionary, Agitator and Labour Leader*, p. 215.
36. *Labour Leader*, 8 June 1906 and quoted by T. W. Moody in 'Michael Davitt and British Labour
     Movement 1882-1906.'
37. *Michael Davitt*, p. 82.
38. Special Supplement with *The Western Journal*, August 1979.

Appendix 1:
An Outline History of the Michael Davitt Memorial Association

By Nancy Smyth

The Michael Davitt National Memorial Association was founded on 9 November 1972. At its initial meeting the aims of the Association, or The Committee, as it is more commonly called, were:

1. To landscape the overgrown area in front of the Abbey and the entrance to Davitt's grave.
2. To bring to the notice of the Office of Public Works the appalling neglected condition of the Abbey.
3. To bring to the attention of the Davitt family that the Celtic Cross over Michael's grave was slanting as a result of a recent storm and needed to be repaired. (His sons had it repaired immediately and we made contact with the family that has lasted over the years).
4. To build a small museum and meeting room in Davitt's memory to highlight the work of Mayo's forgotten hero.

A small committee of nine local people with Michael Howley, as its first chairman, operated for two years out of a local house. The other members of the committee were Kevin Heyns, treasurer, Nancy Smyth, secretary, and active committee members, Nora McHale, Charlotte Doherty, Jack Carney, Michael Kielty, cousin of the patriot, Michael Mulroy and Dr Bridget Heyns. In May 1974, the local committee of nine decided to enlarge the group with representatives from around the county. The late Henry Kenny TD and Douglas Kelly gave advice, with lists of people to contact, and a meeting was advertised on local newspapers. The meeting to enlarge the committee assembled in the Welcome Inn Hotel, Castlebar, with a very large attendance, but it had to be postponed as a mark of respect for those who lost their lives that day in the Dublin bombing. The next meeting was held in Bohola on the invitation of the late Canon McManus, PP, and the association continued to meet there for a number of years.

From the beginning, the association was non-political and non-sectarian and that is still the position. As Michael Davitt was evicted from his home, the aim of the association was to give him a lasting memorial home on a site of land that would be dedicated to his memory. The enlarged committee decided on three objectives to be achieved:

a Erection of a sculpture of Davitt at Straide.
b Building a Davitt Centre in Straide that would incorporate a small museum, a multi-purpose room, kitchen and meeting room on a site as near to his own home as possible.
c Provision of a postgraduate fellowship that would be known as the Davitt Scholarship.

A fund-raising initiative was undertaken. The first trustees were Right Rev. Dean John E. Leeman, Fr. P. Kilcoyne, Kevin Heynes, Michael Howley, William Molloy and Nancy Smyth.

The patrons were: Most Rev. Dr Fergus, retired, & Most Rev. Dr Flynn, Bishop of Achonry, Most Rev. Dr Joseph Cunnane, Archbishop of Tuam, Right Rev. John Coote Duggan, Bishop of Tuam, Killala and Achonry, Most Rev. Dr McDonnell, Bishop of Killala, Brendan Corish, Labour Leader, Dr Garret FitzGerald, Leader Fine Gael, Jack Lynch, Taoiseach, Michael D. Higgins, President of the Labour Party, Professor T. W. Moody, TCD, and the former chief justice, Cahir Davitt, son of Michael Davitt.

The first project undertaken by the committee was to have a brochure designed with a brief outline of Michael Davitt's life, as well as the aims of the association, together with the names of trustees, patrons and officers. It contained five pencil drawings by Liam Swift and the synopsis was written by Peter Filan. The brochure was officially launched in Jury's Hotel, Dublin, in 1975 by the Mayo Association. During that summer, the Mayo Association in Galway organised a lecture by Professor Moody, TCD, in UCG and later at their annual dinner they presented the association with a cheque towards the celebrations. By 1976, a constitution for the association was drawn up with the help of Charles Kelly, solicitor, Swinford, who was also a member. In 1977, the association started planning for the centenary of the Land League in 1979. In 1978, the first site was purchased from the late Jim Roache, comprising approximately two acres in front of the abbey. It was acquired with the intention of erecting a building, but planning permission was refused. A section of the site beside the road was badly neglected and the association had it cleared by Mayo County Council and a lovely landscaped area was provided.

Preparations were well under way for the centenary of the Land League. Comhairle Siúcra Éireann sponsored school projects on Michael Davitt and the Land League for both primary and secondary schools throughout the country. The winning projects went on display in the Imperial Hotel, Castlebar, for a week and they created great interest. The committee applied for the Community Youth Project Training programme run by FÁS, but it was November 1881 before the scheme was approved. The association concentrated on getting radio and television documentaries on Michael Davitt and the Land League. Seán Ó Mórdha produced a documentary for RTE, while the daily papers had very interesting historical features. All this publicity helped to awaken interest in Davitt and his achievements. The first scholarship to UCG was granted to a student in 1978 and a later recipient, Lawrence Marley, completed his Ph.D. To enable us to celebrate the centenary of the Land League, funds had to be raised and this was achieved with church gate collections in every parish in the county and it stands to the credit of local TDs and councillors who helped with the organisation. There was big disappointment when the association failed to get a postage stamp to mark the occasion, but it came later in 1982. From the beginning the association always had the support of the local press and it was very encouraging.

Festivities for the Land League centenary started on 5 August 1979 with the President, Dr Patrick Hillary, officially opening the week of celebration when he was lead into Straide in a carnival atmosphere preceded by marching bands and floats. There was an open air concelebrated Mass with bishops and clergy from the dioceses of Tuam, Achonry, and Killala, and the Church of Ireland was also represented. Afterwards, there was an open-air recital by the army band, together with a celebrity concert and pageant followed by an enactment of the eviction of Michael Davitt's family in 1850. There were over 8,000 people present in Straide on the day. A charter flight of the Mayo Association flew in from New York to take part in the celebrations, and they received a civic reception by Mayo County Council. On the bank holiday Monday, an inter-county senior football match took place in MacHale Park followed during the week with inter club and schools matches. Professor Moody gave a series of lectures around the county while the Western Arts Group, Dublin, produced and performed a three act play written by Gerard Moran on the Life and Times of Michael Davitt. Most of the actors and the producer were members of the Mayo Association in Dublin. The play was a runaway success, being booked out for the three nights it was performed. On the final Sunday there was a wreath-laying ceremony in the evening performed by late Dr Robert Davitt, son of the patriot, and the week was brought to a conclusion with a gala dinner and dance in the Royal Ballroom for close on 800 people. While the weather that week could have been kinder, it failed to dampen the spirit of the people celebrating Ireland's most successful campaign.

40. *Photographed at the conclusion of the Land League centenary celebrations, on 12 August 1979, with Dr Robert Davitt (son of Michael in the centre) and to his left his nephew, Maurice Davitt, were members of the Michael Davitt Memorial Association.*
Seated front, left to right: Fr. Martin McManus, vice-chairperson, Carmel Hughes (PRO), Maurice Davitt, Dr Robert Davitt, Michael Kielty and Nancy Smyth (secretary);
Back row, left to right: Seán McEvoy, Thomas Burke, Gerry Boyle, T. J. Smyth, Pádraic Filan (chairperson), Mary Jennings, Michael Mulroy, John Brady, Seán Reynolds and Kevin Heyns. The photograph was taken in the Imperial Hotel, Castlebar, where the 'National Land League of Mayo' was inaugurated.

The week highlighted the need for a memorial site and building of some kind at Straide as a marker of the birth and burial-place of Michael Davitt and to continue to address his achievements on a national scale. In November 1979, Tara Mines gave a fine donation and this was the start of the building fund. The association organised two more church gate collections, taken up this time by GAA members. After the association drew up a development plan in 1980, they purchased another site adjacent to the existing one from Edward Gallagher. Drawings were submitted for planning permission and fund-raising began in a big way, with celebrity concerts, fashion shows, raffles at home and overseas, a sponsored walk to Pontoon from Straide, and Irish nights every Friday night throughout the county. In 1882 the foundation of the Davitt Centre was laid, consisting of a museum room, multi purpose hall, kitchen, small meeting room and toilet facilities. By now the association were granted a CYPT scheme. The funding-raising continued and Mayo County Council gave a generous grant and it was paid in instalments over a period from 1984 to 1988. The new building was officially opened on 23 May 1884 by Seán McBride, SC. There was great excitement with the new museum, as the association had acquired a very good-sized exhibition of very interesting material. The exhibition was mainly print, photographs, correspondence to and from our hero and some of his personal effects. As the years passed we have acquired more and more items. By 1990, the committee were aware that the museum room was too small for the increased number of visitors. It was decided that I should approach Bishop Flynn of Achonry and see if we could acquire the old church where Michael Davitt was christened in 1846. He gave us the church free of charge. We started fund-raising again.

In 1996, we celebrated the 150th anniversary of the hero's birth. On the 25 March to mark the occasion of Davitt's birth, we had a wreath laying ceremony with the president of the ICMSA, Frank Allen, doing the honours. The ICMSA had their AGM in the Imperial Hotel, Castlebar, and that evening the association held a symposium on 'Davitt the Nation Builder'. There was a packed hall with ICSMA representatives from every county at the function. Guest speakers were Professor Denis Lucey, Head of Co-operative Studies, UCC, Rev. Harry Bohan, R.H.O., Frank Allen, ICMSA, and Dan McCarthy. Also present were two bus loads from the Farmers' Produce Association, Northern Ireland. All the speeches were stimulating and an even more lively question and answer session followed. In June 1996 the remembering continued when President Mary Robinson laid a wreath and addressed a large crowd. A number of visitors travelled from overseas for the occasion including George Burns, grandnephew of Davitt from New York; there was a large representation from the Manchester and Haslingden Democratic Society led by Chris Cleggs who laid a wreath on behalf of the emigrants. The delegation from New York presented a cheque and also the London Mayo Association. In the evening the association had a series of lectures on "The Importance of Land" given by Professor Gearóid Ó Tuathaigh, NUIG, Thomas J. Flatley of Flatley Company, Rolindale, MA, USA, and John Donnelly, President IFA.

Our association tried to mark the various activities and achievements in Davitt's life. On the 8 November 1880, the Ladies' Land League of New York held a farewell meeting in Cooper Institute, New York, as Davitt was returning to Ireland after his fund-raising trip. On the 8 November 1996, the Taoiseach, John Bruton, visited Straide and announced a £200,000 grant towards the restoration of the derelict ruins of the church for our museum, and a research scholarship at NUIG. The funding for the restoration came from the department of Michael D. Higgins, Minister, for Arts, Culture and the Gaeltacht. Prior to the visit, Mayo representative, Jim Higgins TD, who was Minister of State in the Taoiseach's Department, helped in many ways. Mayo County Council gave £80,000 to the restoration along with the magnificent sculpture of Michael Davitt on the grounds. The Office of Public Works contribution was very welcome. Other sponsors were NCF, IFA, Smurfit Limited, Riverdance and the Davitt family, Dublin, who organised a golf classic and raised a substantial sum. The office of the Taoiseach, Bertie Ahern, gave £20,000 towards the audio-vision project. In July 1995, I accompanied an exhibition on the Life of Micheal Davitt to the Irish Festival in Boston and gave lectures there. In November 1996, our patron, Kevin McNamara, MP, organised an evening lecture on the Life of Davitt in the House of Commons with members of the Davitt family and our Association represented.

After two archaeological digs in and outside the penal church, the construction and restoration on the church was undertaken by Deacy & Kielty of Shanwar, Foxford, and it was officially opened by the Taoiseach, Bertie Ahern, in October 2000. In April 2001, John Feerick, Dean of the Fordham Law Faculty, New York, organised a number of fund-raisers for the museum and I spoke at a number of these functions. The audio-visual documentary received an award at the Galway Film festival in 2001 for best short film and was amongst those screened at the Irish-Latin American Festival in May 2002. The association was awarded The Mayo Rehab Award 2001 after receiving the AIB Better Ireland Award in 2000, and won the FÁS Community Initiative Award in 2002 for the Western Region. Members of the association are still working hard to improve the standard of the museum. A heritage grant was received in 2005 towards having archival work carried out on all documents. Geraldine Curtin, archivist, NUIG, undertook the work for the museum over several weeks and provided staff training on handling exhibits and old documents. Every heritage Sunday in September, the museum organises a free lecture for the public, with historians like Dr Carla King, St. Patrick's, Drumcondra, and Dr Mary Harris, NUIG, participating. Finally, I would like to record my sincere appreciation to all members of the Michael Davitt Memorial Association over the years, especially Andrea Wills who has been secretary from 1994 to date.

Note: Nancy Smyth was the founder of the Micheal Davitt Memorial Association in 1972, secretary from 1972 to 1994, and chairperson from 1994 to date.

SELECT BIBLIOGRAPHY

Bew Paul, (1978) *Land and the National Question in Ireland, 1858 – 1882*, Dublin: Gill and Macmillan.
    (1980) C. S. Parnell, Dublin: Gill and Macmillan.

De-Búrca, Marcus, (1980) *The G A A: A History*, Dublin: Cumann Luthchleas Gael.

Boyd, Andrew, (1972 and 1976) *The Rise of the Irish Trade Unions 1729 – 1970*, Dublin: Anvil Books.

Boylan, Henry, (1978) *A Dictionary of Irish Biography*, Dublin: Gill and Macmillan.

Boyle, J. W., (ed.), (1966) *Leaders and Workers*, Cork: Mercier Press.

Cashman, D. B., (1882) *The Life of Michael Davitt, founder of the National Land League* (to which is added *The Secret History of the Land League*, by Michael Davitt), London: R & T Washbourne Ltd.

Clark, Samuel, (1979) *Social Origins of the Irish Land War*, Princeton.

Davitt, Cahir (1979) 'The Treason Trial of Michael Davitt' in *The Irish Times*, 30 April 1979.

De Paor, Liam, (ed.), (1986) *Milestones in Irish History*, Cork: Mercier Press.

Dooley, Terence, (2004) *The Land for the People–The Land Question in Independent Ireland*, Dublin: University College Dublin Press.

Dunleavy, John (1979 and 1983) *Michael Davitt and Haslingden*, Haslingden Local History Society.

Egan, Rev. Patrick K. (1960) *The Parish of Ballinasloe– Its History from the Earliest times to the present century*, Dublin: Clonmore and Reynolds; reprinted in 1994, Galway: Kenny's Bookshops.

Fitzgerald, John and Joseph, (1998) 'Cathedral Cemetery, Scranton' in *Mayo Association Yearbook*, 1998, Dublin: Mayo Association.

Foster, R. F. (1988) *Modern Ireland 1600-1972*, London: Penguin Press.

Freeman, T. W., (1957) *Pre-Famine Ireland: A Study in Historical Geography*, Manchester.

Geary, Laurence, M., (1986) *The Plan of Campaign 1886-1891*, Cork: Cork University Press.

Larkin, Emmet, (1975) *The Roman Catholic Church and the Creation of the Modern Irish State 1878-1886*, Philadephia.

Lee, Joseph, (1973) *The Modernisation of Irish Society, 1848-1918*, Dublin: Gill and Macmillan.
    (1986)'The Land War' in De Paor, Liam, *Milestones in Irish History*, Cork: Mercier Press.

Leamy, P. W. (1946) *The Story of Michael Davitt*, Mayo News.

Lyons, F.S.L., (1968) *John Dillon: A Biography*, London: Routledge and Keegan Paul.
    (1971) *Ireland Since the Famine*, London: Weidenfeld and Nicolson.
    (1977) *Charles Stewart Parnell*, London: Collins.

Hickey, D. G. and Doherty, J.E.,(2003) *A New Dictionary of Irish History from 1800*, Dublin: Gill and Macmillan.

Howley, Michael, *The Rehabilitation of Michael Davitt*, Straide, County Mayo. (It records the celebrations held at Straide in honour of Michael Davitt on 9 June 1946).

Jordan, Jr. Donald E., (1994) *Land and Popular Politics in Ireland: County Mayo from the Plantation to the Land War*, Cambridge University Press.

Kavanagh, Patrick, (1972) *Collected Poems*, London: Martin Brian and O'Keefe Ltd.

Keogh, Dermot and McCarthy, Andrew, (2005) *Limerick Boycott 1904: Anti-Semitism in Ireland*, Cork: Mercier Press.

Killanin, Lord, and Duignan, Michael V, (1962 and other editions) *The Shell Guide to Ireland*, Dublin: Gill and Macmillan.

King, Carla, (1999) *Michael Davitt*, Dundalk: Dundalgan Press
    (ed.) (2000) *Famine, Land and Culture in Ireland*, Dublin: University College Dublin Press.
    (ed.) (2001) *Michael Davitt: Collected Writings, 1868 – 1906*, Bristol: Thoemmes Press.

Moody, T. W., (1945)'Michael Davitt and the "Pen" Letter' in *Irish Historical Studies*, iv, no. 15, pp. 224 – 253.
    'Michael Davitt: 1846 – 1906: A Survey and Appreciation', *Studies* XXXV
    No. 138, June 1946, pp.199 – 208,
    No. 139, September 1946, pp. 325 – 334,
    No. 140, December 1946, pp. 433 – 438.
    (1953)'Michael Davitt and the British Labour Movement 1882 – 1906' in *Translations of the Royal Historical Society*, 5th series, pp. 53 – 76.

(1965)'Michael Davitt' in J. W. Boyle (ed.) *Leaders and Workers*, Cork: Mercier Press.
   (1981) *Davitt and Irish Revolution 1846 – 1882*, Oxford: University Press.
Moody, T W., and Martin, F. X., (1967 and several editions) *The Course of Irish History*, Dublin , RTE.
Murray, James P.,(not dated) *Galway: A Medico Social History*, Galway: Kenny's Bookshop and Art
   Galleries Ltd.
O'Brien, Conor Cruise, (1964) *Parnell and His Party, 1880 –1890*, Oxford Press.
O'Brien, Mrs William, (1937) *My Irish Friends*, Dublin and London: Burns Oates & Washbourne Ltd.
O'Hara, M.M., (1919) *Chief and Tribune: Parnell and Davitt*, Dublin & London: Maunsells and Co.
Ó Muraíle, Nollaig, (1982) 'An Outline History of County Mayo', in O'Hara, Bernard (ed.), *Mayo:
   Aspects of its Heritage*, Galway: Archaeological, Historical and Folklore Society, RTC Galway.
   (1985) *Mayo Places*, Dublin: FNT.
O'Neill, Marie, The Ladies' Land League, paper read to the Old Dublin Society 20/1/1982.
O'Shea, Katharine, (1914) *Charles Stewart Parnell: His Love Story and Political Life*, London.
Ó Tuathaigh, Gearóid, (1972 and 1990) *Ireland Before the Famine 1798 – 1848*, Dublin: Gill and
   Macmillan.
Parnell, Anna, (1986) *The Tale of a Great Sham*, edited with an Introduction by Dana Hearne, Dublin.
Sheehy-Skeffington, Francis, (1908), *Michael Davitt: Revolutionary, Agitator and Labour Leader*, London:
   T. Fisher Unwin. Reprinted, (1967), London: MacGibbon & Kee.
Swords, Liam, (2004) *A Dominant Church: The Diocese of Achonry 1818 – 1960*, Dublin: The Columba
   Press.
Tierney, Mark, (1976) *Croke of Cashel: The Life of Archbishop Thomas William Croke, 1823–1902*,
   Dublin: Gill and Macmillan.
Vaughan, W. E., (1984), *Landlords and Tenants in Ireland 1848-1914*, Studies in Irish Social and Economic
   History, No. 2, Dundalk.
   (ed.), (1989) *A New History of Ireland, Ireland Under the Union, I, 1801-1870*, Oxford University
   Press.
   (ed.), (1996) *A New History of Ireland, vi, Ireland Under the Union, II – 1870-1921*,
   Oxford University Press.

Newspapers: *Connaught Telegraph.*
                  Freeman's Journal.
                  Tuam Herald.
                  The Irish Times – Centenary Tribute, 30 April 1979.
                  The Western Journal – Centenary Tribute, 11 August 1979.
                  Western People – Centenary Tribute, 11 August 1979.

Report
Final Report of Inter-Departmental Committee on Land Structure Reform (1978), Dublin: Stationery
Office.

BOOKS BY MICHAEL DAVITT

Leaves from a Prison Diary; or Lectures to a Solitary Audience,(1885) London: Chapman and Hall.
   Reprint of the original edition, with Introduction by T. W. Moody, (1972), Shannon: Irish University
   Press.
The *Times – Parnell Commission: speech delivered by Michael Davit in defence of the Land League*,(1890)
   London: Kegan Paul, Trench, Trubner & Co.
Life and Progress in Australasia,(1898) London: Methuen.
The Boer Fight for Freedom, (1902) New York and London: Funk & Wagnalls Co.
Within the Pale: the true story of anti-Semitic persecution in Russia, (1903) London: Hurst & Blackett.
The Fall of Feudalism in Ireland: or the story of the Land League revolution, (1904) London and New
   York: Harper Bros.; reprint – 1970, Shannon: Irish University Press.

Note: All these books were published again in 2001. See King, Carla, in this bibliography.

SOME OTHER PUBLICATIONS BY MICHAEL DAVITT

Jottings in Solitary (2003) edited by Carla King, Dublin: University College Dublin Press.
The Prison Life of Michael Davitt, related by himself, (1878), London.
    No copy of the original has been found (source T. W. Moody, p. 586).
    Extracts were published in the *Nation*, 12, 19, 26 February, 5, 12 March 1882.
    Reprinted (1972), with an Introduction by T. W. Moody, Shannon: Irish University Press.
Labour World, edited by Michael Davitt, London, 1890-'91.

Note: For a comprehensive bibliography to 1981 see pp. 579-633 of T. W. Moody's *Davitt and Irish Revolution 1846-82*.

Publications by Mayo County Council

The Story of Mayo, Rosa Meehan
A Mayo Moment: Snow Scenes from County Mayo
Shooting from the Lip: Short Stories from Mayo's New Young Writers.
The Famine in Mayo, Ivor Hamrock.

All titles can be ordered at www.mayolibrary.ie